A Pessimist's Guide to Manifesting

A Practical Approach to Making the Law of Attraction and 20 other Universal Laws Work for You

By

Daniel Olexa, CCHt, ACC

Certified Clinical Hypnotherapist,

Spiritual Laws Coach

And

Iris Terner

Shaman, Behavior Therapist, Spiritual Teacher

and

Reiki Practitioner/Teacher

Cover design and internal illustrations by
Daniel Olexa, Jason Welch @ Earl Design

Cover Photo by msandersmusic via Pixabay

Daniel Olexa's photo by Julie Hopkins at
Camera Creations Photography, Los Angeles, CA

Iris Terner's photo by Dale Chan

A Pessimist's Guide to Manifesting: A Practical Approach to Making the Law of Attraction and 20 other Universal Laws Work for You

ISBN: 978-0692137963

First Edition: June 2018

Daniel Olexa Hypnotherapy, LLC
P.O. Box 3161
Redondo Beach, CA, 90277
daniel@danielolexa.com
310-746-5929

Manifesting 101:

You will never hear
the Universe say,
"It's not you, it's me."

-- Daniel Olexa, CCHt

Image by Felix Mittermeier via Pixabay / Text © Daniel Olexa

Table of Contents

Introduction

Manifesting 101: You will never hear The Universe say,
"It's not you. It's me."

You are in control of your life.

Certainly, there are days when that feels like a false statement. Friends, family, spouses, co-workers, bosses, or maybe the person in line behind you at your favorite coffee shop, are critical of you in some way. In that moment it's easy to feel like an "unappreciated island in a sea of those who are more important and more powerful (those people who seem to have it all together)."

You know those people: pretty much *everybody else* in the world.

Everybody but you.

Comparing your life to theirs, you feel small and unfulfilled. It may seem like all your thoughts begin with *"if only"* and *"I should've."*

Yet, even as these passing interactions draw your attention to feelings of being less-than, you still find yourself dreaming of a better life. In your dream you're happier, richer, working at a different job, or maybe owning your own company (or lots of companies). Life comes easily in the dream. It flows without effort through you. *It just happens.*

What is your experience in real life? Challenges, stresses, personality conflicts, perceived failures, and maybe sadness or frustration that life is not going the way you imagine it should.

Why are you experiencing so much negativity and frustration?

The simple answer: You are giving up control of your life.

A Pessimist's Guide to Manifesting

Whether it is to friends, family, bosses, co-workers, or possessions like cars, homes, and clothes, when you find yourself comparing yourself to others, living the way others think you *should* live your life, or worrying about paying the mortgage, you are giving away control of your life.

This book will help you take it back.

We are here to remind you of your Divine connection to The Universe, your birthright of abundance, and your power as a co-creator of your life.

While this book addresses spiritual concepts, it is designed as a practical, grounded presentation of those ideas. We live in the 3-dimensional, physical world. To make changes in our lives, we need to work at that level, getting our hands dirty by taking action and bringing higher spiritual concepts "down to earth."

In the following pages, you will find individual discussions on each of twenty-one Universal Laws of Manifesting, including the often-misunderstood Law of Attraction.

This book is entitled *A Pessimist's Guide* for a reason.

So many people have confusing interactions with the Universal Laws. They believe that merely by wishing for an event, the Law of Attraction will magically manifest their desire into being. When it doesn't, they think the Law is not working for them.

Remember: The Laws are ALWAYS working!

Sometimes, the timing of our desired manifestation is not about our ego's want for it, but instead about who we need to become in order to fully appreciate, and successfully execute, our goal.

Think of it this way. Imagine that you are an entry level employee of a large corporation. You have big dreams. You can see yourself running this company, or possibly your own firm, yet at this moment, you do not have the knowledge base and skills to succeed at that task.

When you hold that ideal vision as your goal, you can begin to take focused action to learn the skills and get the education you need to become the entrepreneur that you envision yourself to be.

At the moment you are ready, you will set out to realize your goal.

You may even find that since you are taking focused action on your vision, The Universe will have a way of presenting you with appropriate opportunities to gain knowledge faster than if you did not have a goal.

Be open to learning who you need to be to achieve your desires. That "future, ideal you" may have different opinions and ways of being than your current self.

Your ego will try to keep you in your comfort zone because what is familiar is also known and safe.

Your dreams are probably bigger than your comfort zone.

Now it's time to start exploring that space beyond the walls of the familiar.

We ask you now to leave your ego-mind at the door and enter here with hearts and minds open to learning. Some of these concepts may or may not resonate with you as you read them for the first time. You may even be reading about a few of these Universal Laws for the first time.

Practice the exercises that feel appropriate for you. You can always revisit other chapters as you grow in your manifesting journey.

As you prepare to begin your path in the pages that follow, ask yourself, before you begin:

"What do I want to achieve in my life?"

"Who do I need to be to realize my ideal life?"

Allow that question to guide your journey.

1: The Law of Attraction

Five reasons why you think the Law of Attraction doesn't work.

If you are like me, you've read *that* book. You know the one, don't deny it…you don't have to keep it a "secret."

After reading it, you probably fell into one of two camps:

You either thought, "This is great! I just have to wish for what I want! Why have I been working so hard to create a career, buy stuff, and (insert your goal here)."

And you started reciting affirmations about your intended outcomes and desires.

OR,

You thought, "This is bullshit. I can't believe I just spent $20 on this crap."

I was initially in the first camp. I was excited by the concepts in the book and on a metaphysical level, they made sense to me.

But then, nothing worked.

That's when I became a turncoat and stepped into the other group.

The physical reality of my experience was more real to me than the goals of my vision.

I went back to a boring job, accepting what I thought I deserved and I was successful…for a while.

A few years ago, I had a major shakeup in my life. It wasn't so much an existential crisis as it was an awareness of the need to break free of all the stuff and beliefs in which I'd wrapped my life. They weren't contributing to my happiness any longer.

That journey still continues. It's been a challenging climb up the mountain of personal reinvention.

(From an optimist's perspective – more on that later – by being aware of my challenges as I navigate these changes, I'm charting a path by which to help others. That's the realization of my purpose that started me on this course years ago.)

While reading Martin Seligman's brilliant book, *Learned Optimism*, recently, I realized that I am a mild optimist.

What does it mean to be a mild optimist?

On the bright side, I expect things to work out. I take personal responsibility for my role in situations and my ability to find success.

On the darker side, as someone who is only mildly optimistic, I find myself sometimes temporarily overwhelmed by my environment. I fall into brief, false thoughts, hasty generalizations such as, "Nothing ever goes right," "Why do I always have to work so hard?" and "I'm not meant for this."

I bet you've been there too.

What else did I learn from Seligman's book?

I can change my perspective and learn to be more optimistic.

I am a work in progress.

SO ARE YOU!

Over the years, one major realization that I've embraced to help me get out of trash thinking is that over-generalizations are false. They logically cannot exist.

We can think, "Nothing ever goes right for me," but when we turn our focus and begin to look for even the smallest iota of good, we can find it.

And once we see even just one validation of good, we break the absolute of the word "nothing." These realizations, no matter how small, become our foundation for moving forward in a positive way.

Maybe our coffee was perfect this morning, maybe we woke up on time and felt great rather than groggy, or maybe we just saw a perfect sunrise.

While those all may seem meaningless, it's the awareness of their presence in our life that begins to shift our thinking from victimhood to gratitude.

Awareness is an active state of mind. We choose to be aware – and we choose that of which we are aware.

Choose wisely.

Try it. Spend the next week being aware of good things as they happen or reflect on them before you go to sleep. Your opinion of yourself will change for the better.

What does this have to do with the Law of Attraction and why most people seem to struggle with it?

Because your outlook determines what you attract.

If you're a pessimist, or have pessimistic tendencies, you will not look for the signs that things are moving in the right direction. Instead, you'll perceive the obstacles.

Or, deep down, due to low self-esteem, you may not believe that you deserve to achieve your goals and will self-sabotage your efforts.

Here's a list of five reasons why you may be thinking the Law of Attraction doesn't work for you. See if you identify with one or more of them.

1. You aren't clear on your goals

You say you want one thing (a better job, more money, a better relationship…), but you aren't defining what those things will look like.

If this resonates with you, take time to clarify the specifics of your outcome, but don't allow yourself to be bound by them. (We'll discuss that later in the Law of Allowing).

How will the job be better? Shorter hours, weekends off, better environment, better alignment with your skills?

How much more money would you like to earn?

What about the relationship with your co-workers and employer? Will they be more collaborative, more supportive, more aware of your unique contributions to the team and business?

Write these goals clearly and define them outside of temporary fixes, such as "I just need a new job," or "I just need to make more money."

After finding a new job, many discover that the same problems that drove them from the previous position still exist in the new opportunity.

That's because they weren't clear on what they sought to change regarding the larger picture for their new job and the changes within themselves that may be necessary to achieve that goal.

They didn't properly define their vision of their outcomes.

Stating, "I want to earn more money in my job," is not a clear goal.

Instead, use the ideas above to create clarity in your vision for your intended outcome: "I will earn $_____ per year in my new job as a JOB TITLE with a company that supports my personal development that is in alignment with my Highest Purpose and happiness by DATE."

2. You don't want to do the work

W-O-R-K.

WORK is probably the most offensive four-letter word in the English language.

Doing work implies getting results. It's pretty basic Newtonian physics.

Newton's Third Law states that for every action, there has to be an equal and opposite reaction. In other words, if you are taking focused, intentional action toward your goal, you will succeed.

It may not happen as soon as you want it to, but it will happen if you continue to do the appropriate work to make it occur. (Notice Newton didn't say *when* the equal and opposite reaction would take place. He simply stated that it would happen.)

Unfortunately, we often think that the work will be easier than it turns out to be.

If we're pushing against the wall of our goals, shouldn't our goals be responding?

When we don't see results in our imagined timeframe, we begin to believe we are wasting our energy and efforts. So, we stop striving and go back to surviving and struggling.

When looking at the lives of celebrities, friends and family we may judge their success as "overnight," or possibly as "undeserved," because we don't see the years of work that they dedicated themselves to in an effort to realize their success.

Wishing is easier than working. That's why that book I mentioned earlier was so popular.

Admittedly, it worked for some people. Others, however, were left struggling with an unclear path forward.

If you've read this far, you are probably one of the latter group and you want answers.

That's why we wrote this book.

3. You are afraid of failure or success

Let's revisit the idea of the above subject regarding celebrities, friends and family.

When you think about their success, what do you feel?

Do you feel that they didn't deserve it, or maybe that they're too successful: that they have too much money, stuff, popularity, blah, blah, blah?

You're probably thinking, "If I had what they have, I'd make a difference in the world," or "I wouldn't flaunt my wealth like they do. It's distasteful."

I'm here to call you on your bullshit right now.

If you feel this way toward successful people, then you are projecting your own fears onto them. Perhaps, internally you do not feel deserving of success.

You most likely don't know these people beyond news stories about them. In that case, your opinion about them is based not on actual interaction with them, but on an experience mediated by the source of the story and from your own personal beliefs and values about how things "should" be.

Maybe, internally, you don't feel deserving of success.

It's understandable to feel afraid of failure – that's a position that is ingrained in our cultural psyche. Failure is thought to be bad.

But growth comes from failure.

When you were an infant learning to walk, did you immediately move from lying flat on your stomach or back into toddling through the house?

18

Probably not. You experimented first with sitting upright, falling down a number of times until you discovered balance in this new position.

You repeated this learning process as you began to stand and create muscle memory in your legs and core.

You fell down. *BOOM* and learned what not to do.

Then you began to move and walk. BOOM again, many times.

But you survived and learned, created new neural networks in your brain to facilitate your idea of walking, of mimicking your parents' mode of transportation.

Eventually, you stopped falling down, learned to move even faster as your reflexes became programmed with embodied memories of balance and speed.

That's when you began to run.

We learn how to move forward and navigate a new path toward success through learning what not to do.

On creating the light bulb, Thomas Edison said, "I have not failed. I've just found 10,000 ways that won't work."

His resilience came from learning from his errors and shifting his course for the next experiment.

Many of us, when faced with perceived failure, go back to the same course of thinking and try again. Repeating the same process over and over, expecting different results. That's the stereotypical definition of insanity.

The more insidious fear that holds us back is the one that is the hardest for most of us to accept for ourselves, which is the fear of success.

What? Fear of success, you say?

I can hear you now, "Why would I be afraid of succeeding? Of course, I want a better relationship/job/life. Are you nuts?"

Let me ask you, what does this success look like?

Yeah, there's the gilding on the surface – more money, more fame, perception of an easier lifestyle, but look closer…what's under it?

Possibly more work, more responsibility, being in a new position with which you are unfamiliar, more exposure, reduced family time, or maybe less personal time for yourself.

Snapshot summary: Success may place you outside your comfort zone. That's scary.

So, yeah, you can *want* success, you can image it and think of all the wonderful things that it will bring to you, but fear can hold you back, because:

4. Emotion is more powerful than thought

While you may have a *thought or idea* of what you desire, there's an *emotion* behind it that's more powerful.

Maybe that idea was created from a moment of anger or frustration when you realized that things had to change and you wanted a better life.

Maybe that idea was created from a place of peace within you when you had a quiet epiphany on a certain way to bring improvement to the world.

Either way, our emotions drive the manifesting process, not our thoughts.

Dig deep into your ideas. Ask yourself what's driving them and get a sense of the emotions that are associated with your goals.

A sense of fear, or a belief that we are undeserving of success, will hold us back from achieving it.

It will look like the outside environment is conspiring against us, but, in a very real sense, we are sabotaging ourselves.

At that moment of sabotage, we are fulfilling the Law of Attraction by drawing our belief of lack and sense of undeserving to ourselves.

In that way, it's not that the Law of Attraction isn't working, it's that we're sending the wrong signals.

The Law is always working. It's what we're asking for, or what we are unconsciously saying we deserve, that is controlling what is arriving for us.

If you want to succeed and reach your goal, stop sending the Universe mixed signals.

5. You're stuck in the past, defining yourself on who you were, not who you are now

Are you the same person you were when you were five years old?

Unless you are a six-year old reading this, I hope not. And even then, you've probably changed a bit.

Who you learned to be in your childhood is the template from which you decide what you deserve in life.

If you were continually told that you were bad, didn't deserve anything nice because you always broke your toys or thought that because you received second-hand clothing from your siblings you weren't good enough for new things, you might carry a subconscious belief that you can't have a better life.

Even though you've been very successful in many ways, you still see a goal that is *ahead of you,* unachieved. Rather than

21

focusing on how far you've come, all you see is how far you have yet to go.

To realize your future, it's time to let go of the script of the past.

You are no longer the person who you were as a child, or even who you were ten, five, or two years ago.

You've grown. You've learned. You've succeeded at some things.

You're still here and there's still fight left in you.

It's time to change.

Let's examine where you are and what's holding you back.

From the side of the mountain, rather than from the top, this book is here to give you our perspective.

Handing off ropes, pointing out loose rocks and suggesting solid hand-holds, we're here with you. We were once where you are now and we're still climbing.

Let's create a new path rather than repeating the old, familiar ones.

2: The Law of Pure Potentiality

How do you become that which you are not yet being?

There's a quote I love from one of my favorite authors. Iris Terner and I used it as the intro to our book, *Practical Manifesting.*

Neil Gaiman wrote one of the most important things I have ever read.

It will also be one of the most important things YOU will ever read.

Here it is:

"We all – adults and children, writers and readers – have an obligation to daydream. We have an obligation to imagine. It is easy to pretend that nobody can change anything, that we are in a world in which society is huge and the individual is less than nothing: an atom in a wall, a grain of rice in a rice field. But the truth is, individuals change their world over and over, individuals make the future, and they do it by imagining that things can be different.

"Look around you: I mean it. Pause, for a moment and look around the room that you are in. I'm going to point out something so obvious that it tends to be forgotten. It's this: that everything you can see, including the walls, was, at some point, imagined."

– Neil Gaiman

I hope that the weight and importance of that statement is not lost on you.

If it is, let me help you to catch up.

Everything you see in the world, literally EVERYTHING, did not exist physically before it existed as an idea; before it was just a thought.

The doors and windows to your room, the television show to which you give otherwise productive hours of your life, and even this book, did not exist prior to them being an idea.

If you wish, we can take it a bit further and say that the universe did not exist before God had an idea for it and famously said, "Let there be light."

(FYI – exactly who said that and why is up for debate. We'll get to it later. Much later. We're not ready for that discussion yet.)

For a moment, let us set our religious/spiritual beliefs aside and just look at what is; what exists in this physical world.

Let's ask:

1. Why is it here?

2. Where did it come from?

Answers:

1. It's here for us.

2. Someone imagined it and then made it real.

Where did the ideas for it all come from?

They all came from the Universe of Pure Potentiality.

Pure Potentiality means that anything, literally anything, can exist or be brought into existence.

Of course, the means for it to come into existence must be present, such as the technology to create radio, television, the Internet, the iPad, and the ability of man to travel safely into space. Yet, each of these ideas preceded the creation of the technology necessary for it to exist.

That leads me to a common misconception of manifesting.

Just because you want it now, doesn't mean you're going to get it now. (That phrase could actually be the subtitle for this entire book.)

Wanting and wishing aren't enough to co-create. They are merely stones in the foundation of manifesting which must be applied appropriately. This book will lay out additional stones for you to be aware of so that you can build a solid base for your desired outcome.

Back to the concept of Pure Potentiality...

What is it that you want to manifest? How do you feel about it? Do you think you can do it? Are you afraid of what may happen if you do (such as increased responsibility, or the possibility of failure)?

I'll ask you again: Do you think you can do it?

We're here to tell you that you can.

The bigger you dream, the more clearly you can visualize your outcome, the more likely you are to achieve your goal. (NOTE: I am not saying it will necessarily be an easy path, but you will surprise yourself at your ability to achieve grand things when you choose a big goal over a tiny one. Big goals are also much more satisfying to achieve.)

What has to happen for your goal to become real? Like the technology for television, what things need to happen for your ultimate outcome to be realized? Set these smaller items as benchmarks on your path.

Another view of potential

Here's another way to look at Pure Potentiality:

What exactly does it mean to "have potential"? To help frame that question, fill in the blank below.

"My friends/family/teachers tell me that I have the potential to be a great _____."

So, what does it mean to have potential in the role that you wrote above?

IT MEANS YOU ARE NOT BEING THAT THING CURRENTLY.

If you have the potential to be something, you are not yet being it. Otherwise, you would have re-written that sentence as "I am a great _____."

For giggles, and to get a baseline of where your mindset is currently, fill in that sentence too.

Who/what are you being currently? Is it in balance with what you have potential to be? Is it in harmony with your larger purpose for your life?

If it isn't, then it's time to start making changes.

Let's break it down a little.

If you said something like, "I am a great salesman," do you find enjoyment and fulfillment in that role? Is it something you look forward to doing, or is it just a paycheck that's a means to an end?

Maybe you love music and play an instrument. Your friends tell you that you have the potential to be a great musician. Maybe you've thought about putting together a band and beginning to play in public.

Is your current role helping you to move toward realizing that outcome? Do you want to be a musician?

In a Universe of Pure Potentiality, if you have the vision to become a musician, you can do it. (As long as you do the work required to make it happen because wishing alone won't make it real.)

I suggest defining your image of what success as a musician looks like – is it playing in public just for exposure; is it publishing your first single; is it getting a recording contract and becoming internationally famous?

These questions are critical in manifesting your outcome. You must be clear on what it is you wish to achieve.

As we've already learned, the bigger you dream at this stage of the game, the greater your future success will be. Don't play small here – shoot for the moon and beyond.

On my vision board are the words, "New York Times Bestselling Author."

They are not there out of arrogance about my writing ability. Those words resonate with me as a higher level of achievement. They are the potential of that future version of myself that I am working to manifest. (As I am writing this chapter in April 2017, I am not, at this moment, a NY Times Bestselling Author. That role exists as Pure Potential.)

I can see myself in that role and I can feel the emotions that surround the success and awareness that come with achieving that distinction. Feeling is key to the Law of Attraction.

Those emotions are key to manifesting. We will discuss the impact that your emotions have on realizing your future in an upcoming chapter.

For now, your next step is to think about your goals and what brings you happiness. What things do you enjoy doing and what is your picture of your perfect life?

Iris' Insights:

Emotional Mindfulness Exercise

Sit comfortably and focus on your breathing. Relax. Feel each breath in and out allowing you to become more relaxed. Imagine in your mind's eye that you are in a movie theatre. You are all alone but are comfortable being alone. Light flickers onto the screen and a movie starts playing. It is a movie about a week in the life of YOU.

While you watch this movie, observe the different emotions that arise. Do not get involved with the emotions, just make a mental note of them, whether they are good, bad or neutral, such as boredom, indifference, etc. When you are done watching the movie, take a deep breath or two and open your eyes when you are ready.

Now write down the emotions that you observed.

Sit comfortably and focus on your breathing again. Relax as you did before and find yourself in a movie theatre alone once more. Light flickers onto the screen and a movie starts playing. It is a movie about a week in the life of YOU, but you are now living the life you wish. You have discovered your potential and have embraced it and all that comes from it. Again, observe your emotions while you watch this movie and make a mental note of them, whether they are good, bad or neutral. When you are done watching this movie, take a deep breath or two and open your eyes when you are ready.

Now write down the emotions that you observed.

Compare the emotions observed during both movies. Then you decide which life and emotions you would like to experience and live.

The past emotional energy is ingrained within the body and psyche, most of which is negative. Negative emotions create a greater impact upon you, imprinting deeply within, impressing that which is incorrect and fear-based. When the old emotional residue is dealt with, by releasing it and replacing it with emotions you wish to experience, such as love, compassion, etc. in the now, you heal and can move on to live your potential.

Positive emotional balance is not merely happy thoughts and rainbows which ignore the negative feelings. It is the baseline, the balance to which you need to prompt yourself to go to and stay in once the negative emotions are accepted, processed and released. Realize your feelings, reason why the emotions are there, *i.e.,* learned emotional IQ, abuse, abandonment, etc.; how the emotions came about, *i.e.,* triggered by an event or a person; release them - you have a choice of what to feel; recover balance and repeat when needed. Remember the five "Rs" of this healing process:

Realize, Reason, Release, Recover, Repeat as necessary.

A Pessimist's Guide to Manifesting

3: Law of Deliberate Creation

Why it's good to be selfish when you know what you want

I realized that I was playing it safe instead of playing to win.

Winning meant more stress, longer hours, more work at my job – dealing with a variety of needs from advertising clients who didn't care what it took to get it done, it just…needed…to…be… DONE!

I was earning a good living. My stress level was higher than that of most of my friends. I thought that meant I was successful. It certainly meant, to me, that I was important and strong – if I could handle this strain as everyone around me said, "I don't know how you do it," then I must be special.

What it really meant was that I was putting the needs of others before mine. I was misguided and had no vision for my life, or, maybe more correctly, I wasn't connected with a big vision for my life. I thought my employers would take care of me when I showed my dedication.

Oh, they gave me a trinket of appreciation, maybe a small bonus each year, but it wasn't something on which I could build a secure future. It was merely a token of appreciation that kept me locked in an otherwise frustrating role.

Positive feedback is powerful.

You can remain trapped if you are not living intentionally with a personal goal in mind. Positive feedback in the workplace can keep you trapped in a comfort zone of non-achievement.

It's amazing how easily we can wipe out months of frustration with the acceptance of one small note of recognition. It's like our inner voices say, "Look, I told you they will take care of us!

31

They just proved it. Keep doing what you're doing and next year they'll give you even more!"

And of course, the next year came and nothing changed…

This cycle also meant was that I was building someone else's dream for them, not building my dream for me.

Oh, I was getting paid (and paid well), but I wasn't satisfied.

Instead, I ultimately realized that the only vision for the future that matters is a personal one.

Sounds selfish?

It is.

I am.

And you should be too.

When we live our lives primarily based on the needs and wants of others, we give up our goals and our personal power. We live by default, much of it based on our past programming.

Who did we learn to be? What messages did we internalize as children on how we should treat others? How deserving do we believe we are to achieve our goals?

If you are like me, you were told that you were supposed to respect others (a positive thing), but unfortunately the way I learned that lesson meant that I was supposed to make others happy at my expense. I learned that my dreams had no value and I was unworthy and undeserving of pursuing them. I believed that my main reason for existing was to keep the peace.

Over years of repetitious exposure to this message and the positive feedback I received by sacrificing my goals for the happiness of others ("Thank you. You're so kind…"), contrasted with the negative feedback I received when I placed my needs first ("I can't believe you're so selfish! Don't you care about me?"), I internalized the message that I was not deserving of my own goals and life path.

Only recently, after decades of self-discovery have I shifted that belief into a positive one that empowers me while also helping others to grow.

What changed?

Many things – the first of which was I broke out of my comfort zone and put myself first and moved out of a stalled relationship. This was not an easy step. It was quite emotionally painful actually. Thankfully, I had a wonderful counselor who helped me to navigate the path and remain true to my goals for my happiness.

From that moment, I began living intentionally to define and realize my objectives.

This is where the Law of Deliberate Creation comes in.

When we are working within this Law, we are:

1. Accepting of what is,

2. Aware of what was, and

3. Choosing our personal course with intention.

Let's break this down based on my revelations.

What is true for me now: I enjoy helping and empowering others to achieve their success. It's my purpose and passion.

What was true for me in the past: I had learned to put the needs of others first; that I was not deserving of achieving my goals.

Choosing my own path with intention: I can help others without giving up my goals. I can actually help others and achieve my goals at the same time as long as I do it with intention. Since I faced similar challenges and overcame them, I have both the empathy to understand someone else's pain as well as the knowledge of the path to become free of it.

My challenges thus become my strengths.

If I continued to frame them as struggles, I would remain in a fighting mode. As soon as I accepted the lessons and power that came from them, I was able to empower myself and others.

I discovered that I am deserving of my goals – that the negative thoughts in my head were merely echoes of my childhood when I had very little personal power.

Those thoughts have no place in my adult life.

You may have similar thoughts. Please know that they have no place in your adult life either.

If you are hearing or sensing thoughts that tell you that you do not deserve to achieve your goals, ask yourself where they came from and who they sound like. This may be a clue about where you learned these self-deprecating beliefs.

You probably internalized them, like I did, as a child. That is when we are most impressionable and our subconscious soaks up messages that act as a foundation for our beliefs about ourselves and ultimately how we live our lives.

These thoughts no longer have a place in your life. It's time to move beyond them. You are no longer five years old. You have learned a lot since then. You've grown physically, mentally and emotionally.

Stop acting like a five-year old.

Deliberate creation requires you to be an adult, or at least mature in your outlook.

You are not a slave to your past. As noted earlier, the things you learned then can be used as a foundation on which to grow now. What positive lessons can you take from them? How can you help yourself and others by embracing what is, rather than battling against reality because it's not what you want?

When we struggle against what is, we just create more struggle and suffering, surrounding ourselves with a deeper, pessimistic ocean of what we're fighting to change.

You need to stop living in the default mode of your comfort zone that was created by the beliefs of what you thought you deserved to achieve or not achieve.

Your comfort zone is based on the past, not on the present. This barrier will only hinder your achievements in the future.

Deliberate creation requires that we shake things up, that we consciously choose our path.

Deliberate creation means acting on a plan for your life.

Do you have a plan, or do you just have an idea of what would be nice to achieve?

Without an action plan, dreams are just dreams – ethereal phantoms that tease us by showing us what our lives are not.

We can make these ideas real in this world by taking action.

When you are finished reading this chapter, take a few moments to sit quietly and focus on your goals. Think about what you want to achieve – maybe you have an image in your mind, or a feeling in your heart about what your ideal life would be like.

Write it down. Include as many details as possible to make it more real.

Do not edit this vision backwards – do not allow the negative thoughts to reduce the size of this vision.

For example, if your ultimate outcome is to help one million homeless people to find jobs and homes, do not let the voices of your comfort zone say, "You can't even help the homeless guy on the corner. What do you know?"

Embrace your vision and know that all outcomes require a starting point and a process to become fully realized. Be bold, do not shrink from your responsibility to yourself here.

Your action for this chapter is this: **Begin today.**

Become consciously aware of what you are *attracting* into your life.

Are you living just to fill the day and receive a paycheck? Or, are you living with a goal in mind, living intentionally, to realize a dream/desire/goal that is fulfilling to you?

If you have never thought about the difference between the two, start now.

Write down your outcome – dream big. If you can dream it, you deserve it. (And remember the Law of Pure Potentiality – it can happen.)

Ask yourself, "Realistically, how long should it take me to achieve this?" Then reduce that number by ten or twenty percent. You can achieve it faster than you think.

From this moment forward, choose to live your life deliberately to create this outcome. Every day, place as much time and energy as you can into realizing your goal.

What do you need to accomplish first? What event will tell you that you are on your path?

You are deserving of your goal. It is your purpose for this lifetime on Earth.

Go and do it.

Iris' Insights:

To amend negative thought patterns from the past and develop a positive feedback objective regarding your goals, you need to change the story by over-riding the past conditioning. All thoughts, emotions, and speech coming from this old conditioning are involuntary. When you examine this, you will note that what is said and thought is automatic due to past conditioning.

Usually if you stop to purposely think and say something you become tongue-tied and it becomes difficult to pull your thoughts together. Over the years throughout your childhood, teen years and into adulthood, you have been trained to depend on autopilot through the conditioning of the outside world. Most thoughts are negative, based on fear and other negative states of mind which also arise from fear.

Change, Create, and Be Conscious Exercise

We give life meaning. Everything, person and situation has no significance until it is named. That is why people have differing opinions regarding the same things. Create a Positive Feedback Objective (PFO) through re-writing the old conditioning and replacing it with new meaningful goals that you would like to live.

Your homework is to narrate a story you wish to live, pretend you are writing a script for a movie. First, narrate your life now. Stop to do this a few times during the day in the third person. For example:

"Well, look who is getting ready for work. She sure looks and feels excited, not! Why? She is stuck in a rut; day to day it is the same old grind. She gets up around the same time and eats the same food for breakfast and hurries out the door, as she is usually running behind."

Change the story to the life you would like to lead, such as:

37

"Look who is getting ready for work. She sure looks and feels excited! Why? She loves her work. It is exactly what she always wanted to do. She gets up around the same time and eats the same food for breakfast and hurries out the door, because she can't wait to begin the day."

When you start changing the narrative about the job you do not like, also think about how appreciative you are for this job. It puts food on the table and gas in the car and gives you some purpose, because no matter what you do for a living, you are helping others in some way.

Later in the day, you may have the opportunity to write a funny narrative regarding an uncomfortable or bad situation. In the story, make yourself the hero/heroine when you have provided assistance to someone, but do not let it go to your head.

This is not an exercise in inflating your ego self. This exercise is to build greater self-awareness and self-confidence by seeing what you must change in yourself and to remind you what your strengths may be.

You will begin to feel that you are the creator of your life. You will feel happier and more alive. Writing your daily script is also a great deal of fun.

Your PFO will soon root itself within your mind as you develop it and add new parts of the script. It will become second nature, like riding a bicycle or driving a car. You may still be on autopilot, but now the "driver" will be your new PFO. You can create a vision for a new and better life through this exercise and, ideally, become more aware of what you are creating at all times.

4: The Law of Repetitive Effect

Why you are getting what you don't want, over and over and over and over...

"You're stupid."

"You'll never get ahead."

"You suck."

"You can't win, so why even try?"

"What makes you think you're so good?"

Have you heard similar voices in your head?

Lots of us do. I did.

What are these voices that tell you how horrible and undeserving you are?

You've probably found that, over the years, they've been right on many occasions.

Or, actually I should say, *you've allowed them to be right.*

These negative inner voices are just an expression of the old story that we've learned and accepted about ourselves. (See exercises in the previous chapter to create a new, positive story.)

We create these stories early in childhood as we begin to define events based on emotional judgments rather than as mere events.

Here's an example of what I mean: Let's imagine a pair of twin newborn siblings. They begin crying in the middle of the night.

Sibling #1's crib is closer to the door than sibling #2's crib. (Incidentally, sibling #2 started crying first.)

When the parent enters the room in a sleep stupor, they instinctively take the path of least resistance to stop the crying and pick up Sibling #1 because s/he is closest.

The first time this happens, sibling #2 makes a note of it and begins to form a story that the parents must love sibling #1 more because they take care of him/her first.

Over the years of toddler-hood, this scene is repeated many, many times.

As it takes place again, and again, and again, sibling #2 forms a story from his/her observations. It's a negative story about his/her worth that says, "My parents love my brother/sister more than they love me."

Over years of repetition and reinforcement, this eventually morphs into, "I'm not lovable," or "I don't deserve to be loved," as this person experiences the challenges of adolescence and gets rejected for dates or dumped by partners.

We've all been through these situations. They hurt, but why do some people bounce back from them more easily while others dig themselves deeper into a pit of despair?

It's because they, like sibling #2 in the illustration above, are defining an event through a story that has no connection to it. The story that they tell themselves about how unlovable they are has nothing to do with the event of being rejected or dumped.

Instead of looking at a date rejection as, "She's already has plans," or "We have nothing in common to talk about anyway," those with negative self-stories instead define the event as a judgment on their worthiness, such as, "She doesn't like me," or "I'll never meet anyone," or "Why did I bother? No one wants to go out with a loser like me."

And, as these events repeat (as any of us who ever dated knows that they do), the story of unworthiness is reinforced with every single occurrence.

Thus, we become who we tell ourselves that we are. Our childhood creates our adulthood.

My question to you: What are these people manifesting? Are they creating their current life from an idea of the future, or from the experiences of their past?

They will say that they want to date and have a relationship, but their results are repeated rejection.

They want to manifest partnership, but instead are creating loneliness.

Shouldn't the Law of Attraction bring the intended outcome to them?

Why isn't it working?

Initially two reasons come to mind: The Law of Dominant Effect (which we will address in the next chapter) and the Law of Repetitive Effect (which is our topic here).

The Law of Repetitive Effect states simply that the more the subconscious experiences a message, the more likely it is to believe it to be true.

If you repeatedly heard messages in your childhood that related to you being a bad child or unworthy of gifts because you broke things (accidentally, of course) you may have internalized these statements as the story of your value.

You might even believe stories that you heard casually from your parents. Maybe there were times of financial stress in your family during your childhood. Depending on the intensity and number of times that you were exposed to comments about not having enough money or needing to struggle to get ahead, you may have internalized this idea as story of lack regarding your ability to be successful and financially independent.

Through the internalization and ownership of that limiting story, you are now living as the embodiment of the concept of lack.

The good news is that you can change these stories!

The stories of the past belong in the past. They have no place in the present, nor do they have a place in defining your future.

These stories can be replaced in the same way that they were created: through repeated exposure to positive, success-affirming messages that empower you instead of beating you down.

Some choose to use counseling or therapy to begin to break this chain of self-defeating, negative internal messaging. This process takes place mainly on the conscious level and can take years to resolve.

Hypnotherapy has been extremely helpful in guiding clients to turn their thinking around.

This is because the basic elements to our personal stories are held in the subconscious mind. This is the seat of our emotions and beliefs.

By guiding a client into hypnosis and delivering their empowering message straight to their subconscious mind, they can begin the process of shifting their story from one of defeat to one of success.

Recording this session allows the client to listen to the messages over and over so that through repetition, they can reprogram their negative subconscious beliefs into a positive mindset.

It's not always easy. This work takes time – we didn't learn our negative patterns overnight and we don't completely lose them at the snap of a finger. But positive results can be seen almost immediately.

Once in a positive mindset of success and worthiness, we may begin our manifesting journey to co-create that which is truly our goal, and in our best interest.

From a scientific perspective, we can see this Law confirmed in the Reticular Activating System (RAS).

The RAS is a part of our Reptilian Brain. It is an attention-focusing device.

It is the filter that allows a new mother in New York to sleep through the loud sounds of the city yet awaken immediately if her baby makes the slightest sound a few rooms away. Our RAS helps us to focus on what is important and ignore that which is not.

Most people experience the RAS when the buy a new car. Maybe they saw the model on TV and decided, "That's the car for me! No one else in town has one. I'll be the first!"

After buying the car, they see what seems like 20 on every street corner as they drive home.

What's happening here is that, once they purchase the car, it is now in there "sphere of awareness." Now that they are aware of it, they notice it more frequently.

In terms of manifesting, the thoughts that we have about ourselves in our RAS are critical to success. If you are telling yourself that you're failing, struggling, barely surviving, or some other message of lack, then that is what you will be aware of as you live your life.

When you focus on the things that are going right, you program your RAS to become aware of opportunities and you see ways to move forward that you may have missed while you were in a funk.

In short, you create more of that upon which you focus your attention.

For the Law of Attraction to work, you also need to believe that you are worthy and deserving of your outcome. Otherwise, you will sabotage your efforts.

EXERCISES

1. Meditate on your current story. Is it one of personal power or one of self-defeat?

Write it down so that you can become fully aware of it. This is your baseline for change.

2. Meditate on what you want to achieve.

Now that you are aware of your current story, how is it blocking your progress in realizing this goal?

3. To achieve your goal, what do you need to believe about yourself? Do you need to behave differently or believe yourself to be someone other than who you think you are currently?

Do not shrink from this challenge. Remember, in a Universe of Pure Potentiality, you can be and become whomever you choose to be.

Write a new story for yourself, one of achievement, power, success and worthiness.

Remember, you are what you think. Think good thoughts and be kind to yourself.

You are deserving of success.

Iris' Insights

Exercise for Creating Mindfulness

Now that you have created your positive feedback objectives (PFOs) and started to release stuck emotional energy in the last chapter, you can start creating the life you want to live and become the "better you" that you can be with awareness and confidence. The next step is to release the past stories and the emotional hold they have on you by seeing the truth.

The facts, when realized and understood, show you that it was most often not about you in the first place. When the facts are not accessible, you can discern the truth. Using the example story in this chapter: e.g. Did your parents really love your twin more than you or was it just easy access to the bed of your twin that made it seem so? After that story was created, did you assume that everything they did was done without love for you? Do you believe that you did not deserve their love because something was wrong with you? Is this truth or conjecture on your part?

Understand that the facts point too often to something that has nothing to do with "who you are". Seek out the facts for all your stories good, bad or otherwise. These stories form the ego self you believe you are. A "you" has been conditioned by others and you have conditioned a "self" by your beliefs or stories. This "you" does not exist and only appears to be "you." We all create a "you" by taking things personally and creating stories around this "you," which usually are not true.

When you have determined that a story is true, see the "why" in the event. Why did that person hurt you? Discern the possible facts again. Perhaps they are feeling hurt. Perhaps they do not understand what love is. Are they mentally and emotionally messed up? You will be able to see that the fact is that it was all about the stories each person created about themselves. Everyone projects or displaces their feelings and behavior, beliefs, etc., upon each other. Someone wrote you into their story in some way which you then believed and you did the same for them.

After clearing as many stories of the past as possible, envision the life you wish to live in your mind's eye and the new better you. You will need to do this often, as there are many stories that have to be re-written, released and overcome.

When you are ready to create the story about your ultimate goal(s), narrate now in the first person. "I am, I have…(doing this, realizing that, changed this in myself, and now I am like this and so on.) You are not trying to delude yourself. You are writing a script of a possibility that is available and you are stating that you are ready for it.

Be realistic while you are dreaming big. It goes without saying that we all need people to help us in many ways to fulfill our goals. Write in those you know can help you to become the better you such as a therapist, a loving friend; along with those who may bring you resources such as money, knowledge, expertise, etc.

Remember repetition is crucial for this Law to take effect. You have to do the work and allow things to unfold to realize your goals for an optimal life.

5: The Law of Dominant Effect

Why are you afraid of your own success?

In the previous chapter, I mentioned the Law of Repetitive Effect as a possible factor holding you back from achieving your goals.

Here we're going to examine the Law of Dominant Effect.

Simply stated, the Law of Dominant Effect says the strongest emotion wins.

Every time.

That's not to say that a particular emotion, be it happiness, sadness, joy, anger or fear will always win. This Law states that the emotion that is strongest at a particular moment, in regard to a particular issue, will be the dominant force in your ability to manifest your desired outcome.

Fear tends to be a strong motivator in people who are striving to achieve more and actualize their potential.

Fear of being a failure, or judged as unworthy/unsuccessful, motivates us to step beyond our comfort zone.

Fear of success keeps us there.

Ask yourself this: Why haven't you achieved more of your goal? Why are you not further on your path?

You may be tempted to reflexively answer from a victim's perspective that there are elements against you: not enough time, not enough money, not enough _____ (you fill in the blank).

Those ideas are passive. They take your power away.

You must become aware of these emotional reflexes so that you can instead answer from an empowered place within you.

There is always the same amount of time available to us; money is always in a flow; we choose to focus where we spend it; and anything else that you see as an excuse is just that: An excuse.

Active awareness to our circumstances gives us the power to be mindful of our resources and direct those assets in the way that is most beneficial to our desired outcome.

You can always be moving forward. Some days it may only be a step or two. Take time and focus gratitude toward recognizing that any accomplishment toward your goal is forward momentum.

How can I say that? I can say it because I have been there.

I was deeply in debt, without a job, struggling to make connections to network my business, and running out of money fast.

It was easy to feel sorry for myself. The more I focused on not being where I wanted to be, on the things that I sensed were wrong in my life, the more I reinforced the idea that I was stuck.

By reinforcing the stuck-ness, I would tell myself things like, "It doesn't matter. This isn't going anywhere. No one is reading your articles. Why bother?"

Thankfully, I knew enough to slip a little out of my own way and realize that these thoughts were not helping me to move forward.

By staying connected, even in a small way, to my vision for my practice and career, I was able to take actions that kept me moving toward that vision.

And, just in case you are wondering, yes, there were days when it felt like I was wearing 1,000 pounds of lead weight as prepared myself to act.

Rather than lie in bed, I stood up every day I made sure that I did something to realize my goal. I focused on activities that were in alignment with my vision for my future.

I discovered that many of these activities did not have a monetary cost associated with them. They required only a commitment of my time.

This realization moved me past the block that was telling me that I had to have money to accomplish anything worthwhile.

This voice tends to show up saying, "You have to have money to make money." Of course, the implied opposite of that statement is that if you don't have money, you can't make money.

If that voice sounds familiar to you, don't believe it and stop listening to it.

It cost me nothing to do the writing necessary to co-author my first book with Iris Terner, *Practical Manifesting.*

It cost me nothing to research techniques, write blogs, build my own website and create marketing memes using the website Canva.

By creating this foundation, I was showing the Universe that I was (and am) serious about my dream.

More importantly, by taking action, I communicated that I was not afraid of success, because I was doing the work necessary to realize my goals.

Isn't success a good thing? Why would I be afraid of it?

Why would YOU be afraid of it?

You're right – success is a good thing.

In our imagination (and in reality), success brings recognition, financial security and leads us to new opportunities to expand our influence.

But what if there's a dark side to that outcome?

What if the time spent networking and expanding your business is taking away from time with family or friends?

What if your new financial status creates a rift between you and your friends and family?

What if you now have to do hours and hours of reports and tracking to monitor information and staff?

Doesn't increased income mean more taxes and responsibility?

What if, on a subconscious level, you don't see yourself as deserving of success?

All of these questions are based on real fear-rooted situations; situations that are based on our subconscious beliefs and emotions about ourselves.

Fear-centered answers to these questions can keep us locked in our comfort zone.

When we operate from the emotion of fear -- actually from any negative emotion -- we are blocking our ability to manifest our higher good.

In most cases, we are unaware of these subconscious operating systems because they are so familiar to us.

They are our normal state of being for our reflexive behaviors, reactions and thoughts. We stop questioning their existence and validity because they are always present.

However, when we have a vision of our higher good, one that requires us to move beyond our comfort zone of a familiar life, then we begin to push against these foundations of our personal beliefs and stories about who we are and what we are capable of achieving.

You can achieve anything you can dream of. That, as we've already seen, is the Law of Pure Potentiality.

The key is to be more excited about realizing that outcome than you fear the achievement of it.

That's how to use the Law of Dominant Effect to your advantage. When you connect to the feeling of excitement/joy/ success that comes with achieving your goal, you can override the fear that is holding you in place.

Allow yourself to take small steps as you begin this work.

The questions that I raised above are all valid issues regarding how your life may change after you have become the success that you have dreamed of being.

The answers to them may be scary. They are also opportunities for you to grow.

Yes, you may spend more time at your work instead of with family and friends, but you can discuss this issue with them to create balance by forming an agreed-upon expectation that gives you permission to do what needs to be done. Do not be afraid of talking with those who may be affected by the realization of your goal – they should be able understand that you are working towards your dream.

If they don't, then you will have to make a choice between living in their comfort zone with their fears or living for your actualization. Know this: it is not selfish to put yourself first.

Yes, with increased income comes more taxation and fiscal responsibility. Realize that your money flow is from a larger source.

It's easy to think about this from your current financial state and become fearful, saying things like, "I can't afford to pay more taxes."

At this moment, in your current state, you may be right. You have a valid point.

But, if you were earning ten times, or one hundred times more money, the increased taxes are only a small percentage of that flow. In your new state of being, that outflow is minor.

It's time to live in the awareness of your new state of being.

EXERCISES

1. Write down your goals in clear detail. Yes, you've written it down before, but remember, repetition is a key to embedding a message into your subconscious.

2. Now close your eyes and think about all of the complications you can think of that would be reasons why you WOULD NOT want to accomplish your goal. Feel the emotions that accompany them.

Write down these reasons and their paired emotions.

3. Close your eyes again and imagine all the good things that will come from your accomplishment. Maybe your finances are improved, maybe you are helping others through outreach or creating employment opportunities…imagine those positive outcomes and feel the emotions that go along with them.

Write down the things that support your success and the feelings that are associated with them.

4. Compare your lists.

Are your limiting thoughts and fears valid reasons to hold you back from achievement?

Can you see ways to navigate these limitations to overcome or negate them?

When you compare the feelings of limitation to the feelings associated with success, which are stronger?

5. Decide: Do you want your outcome?

After comparing the emotions associated with your goal, do you still want to achieve it?

If your answer is no, then I have two questions for you:

A: Do you want to make adjustments to your outcome that align more closely with your higher good?

If so, write down those changes. Consider this an editing phase to fine-tune the image of your goal.

Repeat the exercise above.

B: If you have decided that you goal is just too much work or that you are not worthy or deserving of achieving it, stop reading now.

It's been a pleasure knowing you. Go back to what you were doing in life and have a good time.

For those who are still reading:

6. Meditate on the positive emotions associated with your success. Do this every day.

The objective here is to associate our powerful, positive emotions and excitement with our desired outcome.

Through this practice of repetition, you are creating the means to increase the association of positive emotions with your goal and negate the limiting ideas that are holding you back.

Limits have no place in your life.

Iris' Insights

Fear is the dominant force in most people's lives. Fear of just about everything, be it good or bad. Our reptilian brains are wired to assist in our survival constantly kicking us into "fight or flight" mode, which is necessary if you are a caveman; not so much for a modern man.

Fear, in all its forms, was introduced to you so long ago you cannot remember the occasion it started, but the impact of the fear is stored within you. Fear is the basis for all negative emotions which go hand-and-hand with negative behavior, thoughts and beliefs. We often become victims of fear as the reptilian brain finds most things, people, situations, etc., to be a threat.

Face your Fears/Anxiety

Get to know fear. How does fear manifest in your life? What is fear trying to tell you? Has anxiety associated with fear stopped you from living your life fully? Where did all this fear come from?

It is understandable to feel discomfort or distress when actively reflecting on the experience of fear. Remember that your emotional experiences are always valid. But, you must confront fear-based emotions, thoughts, sensations within the body and behaviors to change your association with them.

Here are a few fear-based emotions and behaviors:

- dishonesty (lying, embellishing others and yourself)
- anxiety, worry, and/or panic
- being boastful
- depression and/or despair
- fatigue and some illnesses
- negativity in general
- lack of motivation
- excessive focus on the past or the future
- jealousy and suspicion
- not being authentic or real
- being selfish at the expense of others

- pleasing other people
- not standing up for yourself
- not asking others for help when needed
- feeling worthless, helpless or alone
- seclusion/isolation
- fear of success
- not feeling good or smart enough

Be mindful when fear arises. By utilizing the rational working mind, we can examine and over-come fear. Example: Does the fear have a factual basis? Is there an axe murderer actually chasing you? Do you want to be controlled by the fear? You do not see an axe murderer, but you feel you should stay hyper-alert just in case. Is it rational? How many axe murderers are truly wandering around your city? Work through the emotions and beliefs until the present moment truth appears and you find yourself feeling secure and accepting of the truth. "Oh, I am safe. There is no axe murderer nearby."

Once you have examined and accepted the fear, let it go. In most cases, these old patterns of behavior, ways of thinking and feeling serve no purpose, then choose how you would like to feel and behave and think, such as:

- being authentic
- helpful
- empowered
- can stand your ground in an open and accepting way
- feeling worthwhile and strong
- connected with others
- successful
- good or smart enough
- reliable

It is up to you to create your life. Choose to let go of fear in all forms and create the life you wish to live fearlessly.

6: The Law of Experience

Why are you miserable after you had a good time?

This chapter will be a bit different than the previous entries in this book.

Our discussion here does not encompass a total perspective of large events, but rather the final moments of those events. These are the moments in which our memory of the event is anchored.

According to the Law of Experience, the last thing that happens to you in relation to an event is what will remain as your overall impression of the event.

For example, are you going to a party and wearing a new outfit? You had a great time, danced, and laughed for hours, but as you were leaving you overheard someone say that what you were wearing looked stupid.

From that moment forward, you probably forgot the fun of the party and only remembered the embarrassing comment.

In fact, if someone approached you on Monday and asked you about the party, you'd probably temper your review and merely say, "It was OK," because your impression of the party is now tied to a feeling of being hurt.

When we become focused on negative feelings, we limit our experience of abundance. Our awareness, our Reticular Activating System (RAS), focuses on these thoughts/feelings of lack and brings more of them to our attention.

The more we become focused on limitation, the more frustrated we will feel.

From there, we begin our downward spiral of creating a life of shortage. Remember the Law of Dominant Effect?

The strongest emotion always wins. *Always.*

When we apply the Law of Experience to the process of manifesting, it becomes abundantly clear that we must not only become observers of our emotions, but that we must also be cautious about how we explain events to ourselves.

This is important. Let me repeat those two paragraphs.

The strongest emotion always wins. *Always.*

When we apply the Law of Experience to the process of manifesting, it becomes abundantly clear that we must not only become observers of our emotions, but that we must also be cautious about how we explain events to ourselves.

If we get stuck in the emotions generated by our old stories, particularly when those emotions are ones of frustration, anger, or sadness, we get trapped in a place of limitation. Here we tend to see only obstacles, as our RAS is filled with reasons to justify our negative feelings.

If we feel our emotions and let them flow through us, then they have no control over us.

It's easy for us to let our emotions control us rather than just experiencing them, letting them go, and choosing what we wish to feel.

Our ego, fueled by friends who tell us how they would feel (and therefore how we should feel), stays stuck in these emotions. As you already know from previous chapters, if you're stuck in the past, you cannot create your future. Instead, you just recreate the past.

To be observers of our emotions does not mean that we don't feel them. It is perfectly fine to feel whatever you wish to in the moment – anger, fear, happiness, sadness, etc. – but you should not allow these feelings to color the rest of your experience for the day, the week, the month, the year, or your life.

How to Harness the Law of Experience

I recently found myself in a situation where I had counted on someone to help me. When the time came, they were unavailable.

I was pissed.

Thankfully, I stepped back from my anger and took a different approach to the situation.

Had I continued allowing anger to control me and define the event, I would have ruined a good friendship.

Instead, I calmly discussed the situation with my friend and we were able to create a new solution for moving forward that was beneficial to us both.

The positive outcome that we co-created would have been unavailable to us if we (particularly me) had remained stuck in anger.

This new outcome came into reality because we both chose to view our emotions as observers and thus not speak to each other from the old stories that fueled the feelings.

At the end of that day, I felt empowered.

Let's examine this event from the perspective of the Law of Experience:

1. I had a negative experience that I allowed to cause me to feel angry.

2. I defined that moment based on previous (unrelated) stories that I told myself about my worthiness and the uncaring nature of others.

3. Once I realized I was running a negative script of these events, I stopped and stepped back to observe the situation.

4. From the perspective of an observer, I was able to release the anger and other negative emotions that I was feeling. This removed their control over me and allowed me to operate from a rational perspective.

5. Because of this rational perspective, *the last thing that happened* was a positive, supportive, empowering discussion that resulted in meaningful communication and a better relationship.

We co-created a positive outcome where only a few moments earlier there had existed frustration and division.

EXERCISES, PART 1

For the next week, when you prepare to go to sleep, acknowledge at least one good thing that happened in your day.

This is one of the exercises in *The Five-Minute Journal* by Intelligent Change. I do suggest that you buy a copy immediately. It's a powerful tool to shift your mindset from a negative to a positive outlook.

As you begin to associate positive feelings with the end of your day, rather than sensing constant challenges, you'll start to see more opportunities and things for which to be grateful in your life.

EXERCISES, PART 2

Examine your goals and manifesting progress.

As you do, refrain from self-deprecating inner dialogues. Instead, focus on what you have accomplished.

The core of this exercise is to appreciate anything that you have done on the path to realizing your goal.

The purpose of this exercise is NOT to start a mental discussion like, "I should have more done by now...," "I can't do this...," or "It's going to take so long to make this happen."

This exercise is to help you see that you have taken steps (even if it was just to write down your goal – good job! Step one accomplished!) and are now closer to attaining your goal than you may be aware.

Iris' Insights

Meditation on Release of Mental and Emotional Experienced Energies

He who has conquered doubt and fear has conquered failure. His every thought is allied with power, and all difficulties are bravely met and overcome. His purposes are seasonably planted, and they bloom and bring forth fruit that does not fall prematurely to the ground. -- James Allen

Prepare for meditation in a quiet place. Sit in a relaxed position and close your eyes. Focus on your breathing.

Recall your thoughts about some event in the recent past that is plaguing you. It may be a time when you felt you were mistreated, a problem at work or a happy time you wish would happen again that does not allow you to be in the now. Good, bad or mixed emotions and thoughts all must be processed and released; otherwise, their stuck energies control you.

For a minute or so, think in detail about that event. Try to picture what happened as clearly as possible. Be the detached observer while watching this event. Now identify exactly what you are feeling. Be as precise as you can. Do you feel unappreciated? Insulted? Treated unfairly? Over-excited? Or did you have mixed emotions, such as sadness and anger at the same time? Look at the thoughts behind these emotions, e.g., "I was sad it was over and became angry because the relationship had ended when I did not want it to." Or, "I was so happy and less stressed during my vacation. I wish I could still be there. It is hard to go back to work."

Focus your attention on the energy of these emotions and thoughts within your body. Feel where these are stored within the body. You are sensing the stuck energies of the experience.

Be aware that any feelings and thoughts you experience are yours. Memories are not only stored in the mind. They are also stored in the cells of the body. This remembrance can cause muscle contractions, hormonal changes, and other responses within you, which is result of these stuck energies.

Now, for a minute or two, just feel the sensation leaving your body with every breath. Feel that the body is more relaxed and lighter. Sense that the energy within is flowing more smoothly. Open your eyes when you are ready.

While an incident is occurring in the outside world, the effect is entirely within you. You have a choice in how you interpret and respond to emotional and mental stimuli. Recognizing this is taking responsibility for your feelings. This means you have the ability to respond to situations in new ways, which can set you free of the control of emotions and thoughts.

7: The Law of Reverse Effect

Why are you so counterproductive when you work so hard?

Have you ever lost your keys? Your wallet? Your cell phone?

How did you feel in that moment of separation?

Frustrated that you'd be late for work or an appointment?

Scared that your money or identity was stolen?

Did you create stories of outcomes based on your feelings in that moment?

For example, you'd be late for work, get demoted or possibly fired; or maybe you'd have to spend years fighting to reclaim your identity and finances.

Maybe you wondered how you'd function until you had your life back in the palm of your hand.

You probably imagined all of this while frantically running around your home, office or local shopping center looking for that lost item.

Lifetimes of anguish lived in fleeting moments of fear.

Until you stopped.

Until that moment when you took a breath and broke the cycle.

You suddenly realized that unfocused action was not giving you the results you wanted.

You probably took another deep breath and started systematically retracing your steps from the last moment you remembered having the item in your possession.

Through calm, focused action, you allowed ideas and possibilities to flow. You opened yourself to new options that you had not considered while you were being distracted by imagined worst-case scenarios.

Most importantly, you probably found the item.

I'll bet it was either in the last place you'd imagine it would be or it was right under your nose the entire time.

This is the Law of Reverse Effect at work: Try too hard consciously and your subconscious will not help you realize your goal.

We experience the same phenomenon when we strain to remember a name, address or phone number. Focusing too hard consciously on the result, our subconscious (where the information is stored) does not respond.

When we walk away from the conversation, or search, or stop trying to recall the information, it magically appears.

Let's examine how this Law applies to manifesting.

You probably already have a goal in mind. Ideally a big one – one that exists in the Universe of Pure Potentiality.

You're holding the image of this outcome in your conscious mind, thinking about what life will be like when you achieve your outcome.

You take action to make it real because you know that wishing alone will not make it so.

You look for results to show that you're making headway.

But you don't see the results when you want to see them. Perhaps you just see challenges and obstacles instead of progress.

Now you may feel like you're falling behind, or perhaps that the Universe is conspiring against you. Possibly you begin to believe that you just aren't good enough to deserve your dream.

That's when you begin to act frantically, undermining your self-worth with stories of unworthiness that were learned in your past.

Instead of projecting confidence about your outcome, now you're projecting fear and lack.

To overcome those feelings, you work harder, because that's what we've been taught in our Western culture: hard work delivers results.

But your efforts are unfocused and will tend to not deliver the anticipated results, just like when you were looking for your lost keys.

Remember, the Laws of the Universe are ALWAYS working. It is how we work within these Laws that affects how our goals are realized.

Until you embrace the concept of Reverse Effect, you may discover that the harder you try, the harder your work becomes.

The three practical steps to harness the Law of Reverse Effect to your benefit are:

1. Stop trying so hard.

My favorite Zen koan is from Lao Tzu, "Do without doing and all gets done."

Initially, that seems counterintuitive, but it's really not.

When you stop focusing on the effort required to accomplish a task and instead focus on the task itself, your energy flows more effortlessly.

The work toward your outcome becomes less like *learning* to dance (thinking about every movement before actually making it) and truly dancing (muscles moving without conscious thought, instinctively knowing where to go next).

2. Take a deep breath

Relax. It's okay to relax once in a while.

As you do, look at the events that brought you to your moment of frustration.

How could you respond to them differently?

What triggers helped to create your frantic behavior?

Now, from a place of calm clarity, develop your plan to overcome these emotional obstacles.

Do not let your emotions control you. It's OK to feel them, but do not let the feelings overcome you.

Emotions are meant to flow – feel them and let them go.

3. Imagine where you were on your path to achievement before you allowed yourself to become derailed

Just as retracing your steps to find you lost keys, go back to the last place where you felt in balance with realizing your goal.

This may be a physical location, but more likely it is a state of mind.

Connect with the feelings that were present when you held confidence regarding your path: when you had confidence in your path; assuredness in your abilities to achieve, and intuitively knew that your outcome was manifesting.

These feelings come from your higher consciousness that is connected to the Universe.

Our feelings of fear, anger, etc., that result in distraction, all come from ego conditioning.

The process of manifesting is to follow the path toward overcoming the small-minded beliefs of the ego.

It's time to think bigger.

EXERCISES

Your exercise for this lesson is to stop *doing* and start *being*.

If you are stuck in manifesting your goal, take a step back and examine what you are experiencing within.

Are you frustrated and acting frantically in the hopes that *something will just happen?*

Stop it.

Clear away these negative emotions away and begin acting from a state of clarity.

Just allow yourself to "be" for a while. Recharge your batteries and regain your balance.

Then ask your Higher Self or the Universe, "What is the right thing for me to do next?" and be open to the answer.

Iris' Insights

Whenever the conscious mind and the subconscious are in conflict, the subconscious mind always wins.

This is important. Let me repeat that.

Whenever the conscious mind and the subconscious are in conflict, the subconscious mind always wins.

The subconscious is much more powerful than the conscious mind because the subconscious holds the learned lessons and behaviors, which have been conditioned in the past, which are supposedly functioning to keep you safe. Each present-moment situation that reminds the subconscious of a past event is automatically treated according to what was learned a long time ago. This becomes your conditioned automatic behaviors and habits.

The Law of Reversed Effect works in accordance to what was, not what is or what could be. Any conscious attempt to change behavior and habits becomes a struggle as that would mean abandoning what was learned, whether it was good or bad or not. Therefore, when you try to change a reactive response, the subconscious resists. Then it is not so easy to change anything within yourself or in your life. That is why you must step back from the reactive response and note it while entering a calm observer mode. Then you will be able to consciously stop the conditioned behavior and choose to respond differently.

Through meditation, you are able to reach the subconscious and change these responses at the source and re-wire the brain.

Meditation on Habitual Reponses

Prepare for meditation in a quiet place. Sit in a relaxed position and close your eyes. Focus on your breathing. As you breathe, feel yourself relaxing more and more until the body feels very light and comfortable.

Now notice your thoughts without becoming involved with them. As you continue to stay relaxed, allow these thoughts to float by as if they are clouds in the sky. Note any emotions that may pop up. Again, do not become involved with them; allow them to float away also.

Once your conscious mind is more emptied and quiet, you can observe the habits or behaviors you wish to change in the subconscious mind. For example, if you wish to quit smoking see yourself smoking, note the emotional state which accompanies the need for a smoke, e.g., pensiveness, unhappiness, stress and feel the release of these emotions while smoking. Now you feel guilty and horrible about smoking, but the subconscious mind believes that you are in a better state because you released the first emotions and the conscious mind feels the guilt of doing such an unhealthy thing to the body; hence the struggle.

At this point, note that it is a habit from the past that you thought was helping you but it never had. At that time, you may have felt smoking was perhaps keeping you sane or less stressed, but it was just an unhealthy distraction from what you really needed to deal with – your emotions and thoughts. Release all the conscious and subconscious thoughts and emotions driving the habit of smoking. See yourself smoke-free and that you are healthier and happy that you have healed. Feel this and see this, strongly imprinting it into your subconscious mind.

The conscious and subconscious are now aligned.

Repeat this meditation for each behavior and habit you wish to change. Aligning the conscious and subconscious levels of mind allows you awareness of the present moment. This alignment also creates perspective from which you may observe your thoughts and emotions to free yourself from their control.

8: The Law of Allowing

How I Learned to Let Go and Get Out of My Own Way

"I want it all, I want it all, I want it all, and I want it now" – Queen

If you are like me, you are impatient, particularly when it comes to achieving your goals and desires.

There are few things that frustrate me more than waiting for outcomes to occur.

You can probably relate. When we have a goal in mind, we WANT IT NOW!

In our age of digital-connectedness, this mentality is becoming increasingly common. We expect and desire immediate gratification, but is it a good thing?

Allowing ourselves to fall victim to immediate gratification has been shown to lead to reduced success in life. As shown in over 40 years of research by Stanford University, the ability to actually delay gratification corresponds to high social scores and increased achievement.[1]

This state of desire for immediate gratification comes from our mental ability to jump past the work that needs to be done and straight to the idea, "My life will be better when _____," or, "I'll be happy when _____."

If you've been reading this book in order, you're probably going to say, "But wait a minute. Isn't that what I'm supposed to do? See my goal as already existing?"

You are half-right. You are correct that a key to realizing your goal is to imagine it, feel it as though it exists in the present moment, trust that it will occur and live your life as though it has already happened.

Where you would be missing the point is in the nature of the outcome statements above.

Comments such as "I'll be (insert positive emotional state here) when (insert outcome here)" are future-based. They are not focused in the present. In these declarations, the shift of your emotional state is based on an event that is external to you.

What are you really saying when you make these types of statements?

You're saying, "I am not happy with my situation now."

This is what you are projecting as your state of being.

You are saying, "I resist the present situation."

Thus, through a combination of the Laws of Dominant Effect and Attraction, you draw more of this unbalanced condition to yourself.

This frustration and awareness of the present is critical for moving forward. It is our wake-up call to create change in our life.

Unfortunately, many people hold onto this feeling of frustration, which keeps them stalled.

When I hear people say, "It is what it is," they're normally using it as a way of giving up: "I don't like it, but I can't change it." And again, the underlying frustration remains in the present.

If you find yourself saying this, realize that while you may not be able to change the external situation, you are completely capable of changing your attitude towards it.

You need to learn to let go and stop trying to control events and their outcomes.

I'm reminded of the Zen parable of the stone cutter.

The story of the stonecutter is a cautionary tale about losing sight of our own unique strengths and gifts.

In this tale, a stonecutter visits a wealthy merchant's home and sees the affluence of the merchant. The stonecutter desires to be like the merchant, powerful and wealthy. He becomes a merchant to fulfill this desire.

Next, he sees a government official. Envious of the reverence the official is shown, the stonecutter now desires to become an official, which he does.

Now an official, he experiences the heat of the sun on a summer day and wishes to be the sun. It is the most powerful thing of which he can imagine.

Once he becomes the sun, he realizes that clouds have the power to block out the sun and then desires to become a cloud.

Next, he becomes the wind as he sees the power of the wind to move the clouds.

As the wind, he discovers a force that the wind cannot be moved by. Thus, he becomes stone, the strongest material that he can think of.

Now more powerful than anything else, he hears a sound coming from below. He feels his strong, solid form being changed by a hammer and chisel.

Wondering what has the power to change stone, he looks down and sees a stonecutter.

The stonecutter in the story was focused on becoming richer, stronger, more powerful based on external validation. In each phase of his transformation, he saw himself as less-than when compared to the thing to which he compared his strength and power.

It's easy to become focused on our perceived weaknesses rather than our strengths.

When we cloud our awareness with stories of unworthiness, lack and powerlessness, we project resistance into the present. This makes us unaware of our uniqueness and power.

Fortunately, once we clear this resistance to what is and begin to live in a state of gratitude and acceptance of what is, we can begin to change our circumstances.

Here's a practical metaphor to illustrate the concept:

Let's say you are running a five-mile race.

After just one mile, you are tired and think, "Oh, I wish that I could be done already. I just want to rest."

This focuses your attention on being tired and you see the next four miles of running as a chore. Your body will probably feel more tired and achy. You'll stop, walk more frequently and you'll most likely finish the race, but you won't deliver your best effort.

Instead, you could embrace the reality of your tiredness and the remaining distance to create a new outlook where you take action to change your pace so that you have enough energy to complete the race.

In this scenario, you accept your state.

In this new reality, you allowed the existing circumstances and created a winning solution. You did not fuel resistance to the situation.

Here's a recent practical example from my own life:

When I was selling my house, I felt hope with every notification of a new showing; then fell into a funk when the less-than-positive feedback rolled in. I just wanted to feel the weight of it off my back – owning this house no longer served me, my present or my future, but there it was, a monthly drain on my finances.

I prayed, I meditated, I visualized, I asked the Universe to send the perfect buyer...

And then I paid the mortgage for one...more...month.

Where was my manifestation of no longer being a homeowner? Why was I stuck owning a house over 2,000 miles away?

What could I learn from this perceived blockage?

I learned a few things, one of which was patience.

I also learned that things are what they are, and I learned how to work with that reality instead of against it.

In my mind, I wanted a certain price. I knew that to sell the house at that price, I would receive a specific amount of net dollars after the sale. I was focused on the gross number, not so much on the net number.

I was resistant to the reality of the market and the existing condition of a house that I had not lived in for two years.

When I stopped trying to control the details of the transaction, I allowed a new possibility for the sale to exist.

Within 3 weeks, the house sold and, while the total sale amount was not what I originally had in mind, the net proceeds were in alignment with my desired outcome.

Look at that sentence again.

I had based my selling price on what I ultimately wanted to financially clear on the sale.

The house sold for less but, due to the details of the contract, I was left with the same net earnings.

Acceptance of reality is not giving up, nor is it capitulation to that which is outside of your control.

It's actually a way of preserving your energy and using it for what matters (what you DO have the power to change), rather than wasting your energy fruitlessly.

In Chapter Two, we discussed the Law of Pure Potentiality -- the idea that in an infinite universe, all things are possible.

If everything is possible, ask yourself, what are you not allowing in your life? And why?

How are you blocking yourself from achieving your goals?

EXERCISES

Make a list of the things that you sense are in your way. What's preventing you from realizing your outcomes?

Examine that list and shift your thinking. Look for opportunities, ways to overcome these issues.

Ultimately, achievement is your choice.

What exists today can be changed.

You have the power to change it, but first you must accept the role it is currently playing in your life.

Iris' Insights

Acceptance Exercises

Everything is energy. You are in an "energy loop" with All That Exists. The Law of Allowing is working with the flow from the Universe when you accept what is returned to you before it even arrives.

This means you must use the Law of Allowing to accept what you wish for and how it unfolds and becomes. Resistance is not flow. Whether something looks good, bad or otherwise, all things must be accepted.

The best way to practice the Law of Allowing is by simply saying "yes" to things you receive in your life and being grateful for them. Of course, if you don't want something, you politely can say "no."

But *be careful*. What you say "no" to may benefit you in the long run. Be sure that you think about it before you say "no" as you may ultimately need that situation, person or thing. Examine why it is in your life. Is this a blessing or a lesson? Could this lead to something or someone else that could fulfill your goal(s)? Discernment is crucial. Be as certain as possible before making a yes or no choice.

If you need advice, do not seek validation; only ask those who have true knowledge on the subject. If you are unable to make a decision, you may have an emotional block or a belief that is hindering you.

You must then look deeply within to sort this out.

This is when the meditation on habitual responses in the previous chapter will help. Professional assistance may be necessary to find these blocks if they are very deep and challenging.

When you use the Law of Allowing, you are saying that you have no resistance to what you want and the flow of energy will be easy and direct. There will be no stumbling blocks. But you must see what you wish for as part of your life and you must accept life as it comes since you cannot control it.

You can ask The Universe for assistance in fulfilling your purpose, living the best life you can live and finding true happiness.

There is nothing wrong with that as long as you allow The Universe to create the best of what can be, whatever the outcome may look like.

9: The Law of Giving and Receiving

One powerful shift to overcome your fear of lack

The Law of Giving and Receiving is a concept that has caused me issues over the years.

I struggled with finances for much of my life, not quite knowing how to handle money properly, how to fully respect it and, most importantly, understanding how it flows.

When we're on a path of self-reinvention, it is often our financial state that pushes us forward to change. Maybe we're not earning enough money, or feel that we need to do something differently, or we're just not happy with our current state of life.

This dissonance between who we want to be/what we want our lives to be may leave us with a sense that we need to bridge the gap between the now and our ideas of the future.

Yet, it seems that the more we pursue the money, the further away it seems to be. Often our hard work doesn't immediately pay off and we're left wondering if it was all worth it.

In those moments of uncertainty, when we're barely making it from paycheck to paycheck (assuming that there are paychecks), fear can lock us into a mindset of lack where we hold onto every dollar as though it is our last.

Instead of being confident in ourselves and our ability to navigate ourselves out of this temporary state, we project the worst possible outcomes and focus on possible failures that likely do not exist.

Remember the Law of Pure Potentiality? You can create any outcome…choose wisely.

Remember the Law of Dominant Effect? The strongest emotion always wins.

The Law of Giving and Receiving is simple: To receive, you must give that which you wish to receive.

As you probably know, that can be more easily said than done.

If you're in a place of financial hardship, it's difficult to let go of money that could be used to pay bills or deliver food to the table.

Here's the key: It's not about the amount as much as it is about the action of giving.

If you're holding onto money because you are afraid of not being able to pay a bill, then guess what emotion is dominant?

You got it: Fear.

Fear blocks growth.

Now, let me be very, very clear on this point: I am NOT telling you to go on a spending spree and empty the last penny, dime and nickel out of your pocket. That's foolishness.

What I am suggesting is that you find an amount of money that you feel comfortable giving away and donate it to a place that resonates with your soul, a place that gives you "spiritual food."

It could be, but doesn't have to be, a church, a homeless shelter, a children's organization, a pet shelter or any other organization that you feel does good work and that you admire.

I love the way Edwene Gaines addresses this in her book, *The Four Spiritual Laws of Prosperity*. She discusses giving money to a waitress who talked with her while she was having coffee. The lesson she received from that conversation was, to her, spiritual food.

Tithing is rule #1.

Give this money freely and graciously. Do not give it with a feeling of dread or you are reinforcing the Law of Dominant Effect.

It all comes down to mindset. You will see what you choose to see as the outcome of every action. This is where your subconscious plays a vital role in realizing your outcomes. You program your Reticular Activating System (RAS) to be aware of lack or abundance by your thoughts.

If you give with fear, you will resonate that energy of lack and realize it when you examine the results of your gift. In terms of the Law of Attraction, in this state you are vibrating with the feeling of lack of abundance.

If you give with gratitude, you are programming your RAS to be alert for signs of receiving a positive return on your gift, a reflection of what you gave. You'll see opportunity instead of obstacles.

All things flow. To receive, you must give.

All things exist due to the interdependent connectivity of cause and effect.

Day and night, heat and cold, wet and dry are just two sides of the same proverbial coin (just like heads and tails).

Giving is receiving and receiving is giving.

The act of hoarding blocks energy and prevents you from experiencing the inward flow of prosperity.

How does this work?

Let's say you've made some less-than-well-informed purchases over the years. (We've all done it. It's okay to admit.)

When you look back on those items that are now sitting in your garage or spare bedroom, there's a bit of frustration that may be associated with them. Do you ever catch yourself saying, "I wish I wouldn't have bought that…," or "I should have saved that money…," or "I can't believe I spent $____ on that piece of crap"?

If you do, you are again experiencing the Law of Dominant Effect. The frustration associated with these purchases is taking control of your perception of financial flow.

Your underlying thoughts may begin to reinforce old belief patterns such as, "I don't deserve money because I waste it," or "Anytime I start to get ahead, it just goes away. I can't catch up."

Maybe you have been wasteful in the past. That does not mean that you have to be wasteful now. You can break that behavior.

Think of the Universe as a parent giving you an allowance.

If a child is wasteful with his/her allowance, should his/her parent just give them more?

No. That will reinforce the wastefulness.

When a person learns to respect money, then they are entitled to more of it.

If you are showing the Universe that you are a wasteful child when it comes to your attitude toward abundance, then you will experience lack until you shift your actions.

You are perfectly capable of changing your financial situation.

Awareness of your attitude, honesty with yourself, and respect of money are the keys to creating that shift in mindset.

EXERCISES

Examine your financial position.

Are you living in abundance with money flowing easily, or are you experiencing obstacles to creating financial freedom?

What things can you do to change your outlook and your situation?

In terms of giving, from where do you receive your spiritual food? How much are you going to give to that person or organization?

Iris' Insights

In *The Seven Laws of Spiritual Success,* Deepak Chopra stated that the intention when giving should be to create happiness for the giver and receiver.

Everyone deserves happiness.

It is life-sustaining. If you want joy, give joy to others; if you want love, do your best to give love; if you want attention give it. If your goal is to become materially affluent then help others to do the same. In fact, the easiest way to get what you want is to help others get what they want.

Giving and receiving are not only about money or material things. You can also give free services to the less privileged; offer emotional support; donate things you no longer need or want, etc. The important thing is your intention and ability to give.

Search within for ways you can give of yourself without expectation of return from those you give to. Intention should be pure, no ego involvement and no "eye" on the outcome. There is always a receiving end to giving because it is one and the same.

When you put the energy of this purer intent into everything you do, especially when giving, the outcome will always be positive. Allow yourself to receive freely what comes.

"It's not how much we give but how much love we put into giving." — Mother Teresa

10: The Law of Cause and Effect

How Does Newton's Third Law of Motion Apply to Manifesting?

We live in a three-dimensional physical universe. That's where our bodies occupy space.

As a reader of this book, you are probably spiritually-minded and open to the concept of an infinite universe and multiple dimensions. We've discussed this concept in Chapter Two *as the Law of Pure Potentiality.*

In this chapter, I'm not going to concentrate as much on the limitations of the physical universe as much as I am the Laws which currently seem to apply to it. (For the science-minded, please don't cringe at that statement. Scientific discoveries are always advancing. What's accepted now may be altered or discredited in the future as our understanding evolves.)

Newton's Third Law of Motion states, "For every action, there is an equal and opposite reaction."

Ok, you're probably thinking, "So what? Blah, blah, blah…I didn't pay attention in science class and, even if I did, this just doesn't matter to me living my life every day."

Well, Bucky, actually it does.

The effort that you put into your life, into your intentional manifesting work, does come back to you as a reaction from the Universe.

If you're letting life happen to you, there's a good chance you are not seeing your goals come to fruition and you probably feel a bit like a victim of life, because the inverse of Newton's Third Law is also true: for every non-action, there is an equal and opposite lack of reaction.

Honestly, even if you are taking action, there's no guarantee that you're going to see exactly the outcome that you desire, mainly because you may be focusing on details rather than a bigger picture.

But you will see an outcome from your efforts.

As you focus your attention, and act with intention, the return effect on your actions will increasingly be in alignment with your goals.

We can see this same concept in a variety of spiritual teachings.

Wiccans hold this idea as the Three-Fold Law. Essentially, whatever energy you put out will return to you multiple times over.

In the Bible, there is the Golden Rule: "Do unto others as you would have them do unto you." Not quite as clear in its language, the Golden Rule is still presenting the concept that the energy you put out in the way you treat your fellow man will be reflected back to you.

This concept also appears in Galatians 6:7 as, "Do not be deceived: God cannot be mocked. A man reaps what he sows."

In other words, what you put out, you get back…and the Universe (or God, if you prefer) is watching.

How does this apply to our attempts to manifest our goals?

On one level, it applies to our work…that we actually take action to manifest our outcomes. Without action, there is no response.

Go ahead, sit on a park bench and dream about your goal. Until you get up and start doing something about it, you're probably not going to manifest much more than a gathering of pigeons.

It also means that we must be focused, that our actions must be intentional and in alignment with our goal.

For example, if my objective is to run a marathon, the action of binge-watching Netflix every weekend while eating pizza is probably not going to help me become an effective runner of 26.2 miles. But I will see a bodily reaction to my pizza, beer and TV bingeing – I'll probably store the energy as layers of fat.

Lesson: There is no wasted energy. All energetic output will flow back to you as a reflection of that energy.

Eat poorly on a regular basis = experience negative health issues. Become active and train with purpose = run a marathon (if that's your intended outcome) = better health.

If your goal is to have a successful business, how are you applying your energy to that outcome? Are you focusing your efforts to outreach and awareness, or are you surfing Facebook in your spare time?

If your goal is to own a home, are you saving money, visualizing your ideal house and researching places to live, or are you running to the mall (or Amazon) as soon as you hear the word "sale"?

If you wish to create a life of success and abundance, begin behaving in alignment with that wish as you take action. Be of service to others, give what you can where you can and do so with an attitude of gratitude. Keep in mind, it's not only the action, but the energy behind our actions that resonates with the Universe. Remember the Law of Attraction from Chapter One?

How are you applying your energy to manifesting your outcome?

EXERCISES

Revisit your desired outcome. Check to make sure it is still what you wish to realize.

Now, write down three intentional actions that you will commit to take during the next 7 to 10 days. Place dates for completion next to each and hold yourself accountable…because the Universe certainly will.

Iris' Insights

The purpose of mindfulness here is to develop an awareness of cause and effect. The concept of karma comes up in relation to cause and effect. Karma is not punishment, but simply a consequence of actions and behavior. It is the universal principle of action and reaction that governs life. The effects experienced can be mitigated by good acts making consequences not necessarily fated as consequences. Karma can be immediate, delayed, or changed by your attempts. That is to say, a particular action now is not binding you to some particular, pre-determined future experience or reaction.

You must realize that good and bad actions are dependent upon your intent. Your intention is based upon your actions, thoughts and feelings being aligned for a good or bad reason. At times, we can become confused or deluded and thus act with an unclear intent.

Become mindful before you speak or do something and stop your usual negative behavioral patterns. When you become mindful of how you are aligned inside yourself, in a positive, negative or uncertain way, you can act accordingly or choose to change what you believe you need to before acting, creating positive karma or changing negative karma. You can do this by asking yourself the following questions before acting:

Why am I about to follow through with this action or behavior? Am I being reactive or interactive?

What are the thoughts trying to tell me? Are these thoughts negative or positive? Are they from the past? How do these thoughts apply now?

What am I feeling? Are these feelings negative or positive? Are they from the past? How do these feelings apply now?

Am I confused or do my thoughts, feelings and actions line up? For example: if the body is tense, feelings of anger arise and negative thoughts dominate; your intent is negative and will cause a negative effect when acted upon.

If your body is tense, you are uncertain of how you are feeling and confusing thoughts are bouncing around in your head. Nothing is aligned; therefore, confusion and chaos will be the result.

Or, if your body is relaxed and you are experiencing feelings of compassion as caring arises and kind, understanding thoughts are strong, then your intent is positive and will cause a positive effect when acted upon.

11: The Law of Neutrality

How giving up can lead to actualization

"Do without doing and all gets done." – Lao Tzu

We've reached the mid-point in our manifesting/life-mastery journey through the Universal Laws.

Congratulations on your commitment to doing the work.

During the time you have been reading this book you probably have been taking action to realize you goal and you've probably experienced a few bumps in the road of your manifesting process.

Maybe they were intense enough that you questioned your path and resolve.

Know this: Everyone experiences obstacles as we move out of our comfort zone to create a new, bigger life. You are not alone.

Only when we let the frustration of these moments overwhelm and derail us do we lose sight of our calling. We hesitate for a moment as ego takes control and we get stuck in the challenges of the present.

It is now time for us to talk about alignment with our Higher Purpose. We're going to move past the need for personal control and learn to let go.

People who are attached to their outcomes say things like, "I'll be happy when _____," instead of allowing themselves to experience happiness as a core state of being.

The answers that may fill in the blank in the statement above can include, "...I have a new job," "...I have a new relationship,"

"I'm free from my current relationship," and "... the kids are grown and out of the house."

What's your answer to the question of when you will allow yourself to be happy?

Individuals who focus at this level are vibrating from a state of lack. Their goal has not yet been achieved, so they focus on who they are not and what they do not have.

As we know from our discussion of the Law of Attraction, our vibration creates our reality. (So much of manifesting comes back to this Law, doesn't it?)

Acting as if your outcome already exists is one step to realizing it. Be happy first, then accept and allow the objective to come to you. Be a magnet for it.

"But I'm human," you say. "I want to achieve NOW! I'm tired of waiting. This is frustrating."

I hear you. I get it. I've been there.

I had to learn to let it go and so do you.

Our attachment to a particular outcome tends to originate in our ego-mind.

That makes sense. We're taking action to realize a vision of a future. Our actions are based on what we've experienced in this life, so we look toward physical verification of our achievement: more money, happier relationships, successful business, etc.

We think of our outcome as an end-point instead of as a foundation for our next level of growth.

As you may already sense from your journey, there are two big issues with this outlook:

1. These things are all temporary states of being. Once we achieve these outcomes, we find that we're not as happy or fulfilled as we thought we'd be and,

2. They are based on what we think we want at a particular moment in life. As we progress on our journey to realize these goals, we change as beings. As we change, our goals may no longer fit us therefore, we're not satisfied when we achieve them.

Do you see the paradox?

Without a desire to make a change in our lives, we won't take action, but once we take action, then we need to let go of the desire for the specific outcome.

Why would you keep taking action if you have no attachment to the result?

Here's a personal story of how attachment to an outcome negatively affected me:

When I set the intention for my first hypnotherapy practice, I had laser-like focus. The picture in my mind was so real I could almost touch it.

One of the major bullet points for this vision included my practice being the most successful hypnotherapy practice in Southwest Florida. That location was so important to me that I branded my business for the region – even though I was told by those with more experience and insight not to do that.

But I was smarter than they were, right? I knew what I was doing. I had this grand vision. What did they know?

Well, three months after opening my practice, I learned that I was moving to California.

Turns out those other people knew a lot more than I gave them credit for.

The process of closing my business and re-branding took a lot out of me. Mentally, physically and emotionally, I felt as though I had lost my dream.

It took me months to get out of that funk and embrace a new, bigger vision that is more in alignment with my purpose than the ego-fueled foundation of my first practice. This new vision was also free of the limitations of being tied to a specific physical region.

My original goal was not aligned completely with my Higher Purpose. The reasons for its existence were driven by my ego's desire to be important, successful and wealthy.

Ultimately, it was a lesson in ego-breaking that I had to learn.

I had to let go of the specifics of my vision and allow it to evolve to the right outcome.

So, what do we do? How do you let go of your intended outcome, that thing that you want so badly that you were willing to quit your job, give up on vacations and take a second mortgage to make happen? You're vested in this dream… how can I be telling you to let go of it?

Here is where the Law of Neutrality comes to your assistance.

This Law asks that when you are overwhelmed by frustration, just stop acting.

Before we go further, take a deep breath and relax. Here's a quick reference to help put this in context:

I am a PADI scuba diving instructor. When I teach scuba diving, one of the most important things I discuss with new divers is to always stay calm.

This is particularly true in entanglement situations.

Divers can encounter a lot of line in the water: fishing lines, old nets, or maybe even old navigation lines that were placed by a previous diver. They could even be our own navigation lines.

Anytime we're near lines in the water, there is always a chance of getting tangled in them.

If this happens, the understandable first reaction is to try to get clear as quickly as possible. I mean, there's only so much air in that tank, right?!?!?

Unfortunately, frantic action just leads to more entanglement as we spin the line around us (and you use up your air faster than if you stay calm – double whammy).

The proper response is to stop, breathe, think, and act.

From a calm, logical place, a diver can figure out how to best remove him- or herself from a dangerous, potentially life-threatening predicament.

I'm going to ask you to do the same now.

The Law of Neutrality reminds us to stop when we're in a mode of frustration; when we're in our own way and things aren't working out the way we want (notice that word, "want"), step back and view the situation from the perspective of an observer.

"Want" comes from ego – it is personal. It is our small mind, not our Higher Self.

"Want" is based on lack – we want something we don't have. "Want" ignores the experience of abundance.

Stop Wanting, Start Having

Rather than "wanting," instead view your outcome as already existing. More importantly, connect with it on a kinesthetic level and *feel* as though it already exists; believe it.

This seemingly small shift in perspective will accomplish two things: (1) you will move from a feeling of wanting to a feeling of having, and (2) from that connection to sensing and believing that you already have your outcome, you will be working in alignment with the Law of Attraction.

Our subconscious mind does not know the difference between an event actually occurring and one that we imagine. This is why we react emotionally to movies, books, and other non-direct stimuli.

It is also why visualization is such a powerful tool for achieving success. Visualization can create physical changes in your brain.

A study at Harvard Medical School by neuroscientist Alvaro Pascual-Leone compared the results of two groups of piano students. One group practiced a piano exercise for two hours per day, while the second group only visualized themselves performing the exercise.

At the end of one week, a comparison of brain scans of both groups showed that the students who only visualized the exercise had similar stimulation and growth in the area of their motor cortex as those who had actually performed the piano skills.[1]

In your visualization of your ideal outcome, become the observer that the Law of Neutrality requires. Imagine yourself in that place of success, rather than enmeshed in your current frustrations.

When you find yourself struggling, stop moving. Take a deep breath…or two…or three.

Center yourself and ask if your "doing" is in alignment with your Higher Purpose, or is it coming from ego? Are your actions in alignment with your goals?

If your vision of your outcome came from your Higher Self, it is showing you an image of what your life can become.

When we let go of our ego's wants, and listen to The Universe, we allow things to fall back into alignment.

Everything you experience has been placed in your path for a reason. If you are experiencing frustration, stop acting and ask your Higher Self for clarity regarding the lesson you are supposed to learn in your current state.

Become a neutral observer of your life. See if you are applying efforts that are taking you toward your goal or away from it. If you sense the latter, change your actions.

EXERCISES

This time, your work is easy.

Just stop everything and observe your state of being.

You can do this for an hour, or a day, or a week. Your choice.

Look at the areas where you have experienced frustration and obstacles. Ask yourself, from an observer perspective, why they were in your path.

Listen to your intuition.

Iris' Insights

Total Surrender Meditation

A surrender meditation can start with a prayer to your Higher Self, God or whatever is Divine to you. Pray to give over everything, your body, mind, emotions and life, to The Divine or simply hold a pure intent within your heart that you wish to free yourself of all obstacles, behavior patterns, emotional and mental turmoil, etc.

I find it easier to let go of things when I say my prayer out loud. I prepare in my usual way to sit in meditation and then I center in my heart (chakra) and recite:

"Dear God, Dear Spirit, Dear I Am: I totally surrender all ego-conditioning to You; please take all ego-conditioning away and deal with it for this soul. I totally surrender all karma (cause and effect tendencies) of all lives, of others and ancestors to You; please take all karma away and deal with it for this soul. I totally surrender all illusions and delusions of this and all realms of existence and of all dreams to You; please take all illusions and delusions away and deal with it for this soul. Please and thank you."

I feel the energy of ego-conditioning, karma and illusions and delusions lift off me as I recite my prayer.

I will proceed to release all fears, concerns and burdens of responsibilities; seeing responsibilities as not something I "have" to do; they are just part of existence here and what I normally do throughout the day. I then start releasing needs and desires or anything I may be obsessing over. I move on to releasing aversions and all negative thoughts and emotions; anything which may arise.

Then, I complete my meditation by surrendering all effort and striving, all sense of doing anything until I feel that I am a "being-ness" of pure, expansive, higher energy.

Make this meditation your own by utilizing whatever steps suit you. Your purpose here is to empty and quiet yourself – your mind, thoughts, and emotions – as much as possible and to connect with your Higher Self, your "real" self.

12: The Law of Will

Two steps to get out of your own way

In the previous chapter, we discussed the Law of Neutrality. This Law reminded us to stay calm and let go of attachment to our outcomes.

The Law of Will asks us to leave the wants of our ego behind and realize that our personal will is also Divine Will.

This is where you're going to learn how to get out of your own way.

If you've been following along and doing your homework, you've probably encountered some challenges to your efforts. Maybe you felt resistance, maybe you just thought you couldn't complete your task, or maybe you decided that you didn't want to pursue that outcome anymore.

No matter where you are, it's now time to stop and examine your current state.

We're not going to look at how far you may have yet to go. Let's instead look at how far you have come, what you have achieved, and your perceptions about those results.

Looking back at the goal you set when you began this program, what have you accomplished in your pursuit of it?

How do you feel about your results so far?

If you are happy with what you have accomplished, then there is not much need for you to read further. Bookmark this section as a reminder to revisit it if and when you do encounter resistance. For now, you may go look at pictures of cats on

Facebook, jump to the next chapter, or stay focused on achieving your next benchmark.

This specific chapter is for those of you who are not feeling satisfied with where you are in relation to your goal.

Are you hearing the thoughts or voices of negative internal loops? You probably know them. They sound like, "This is too hard," "I'll never get ahead," "I can't do this. Why did I even try?," "I don't know what I'm doing," or "It's already been done by somebody else."

Those thoughts are coming from an ego-based story that you learned and internalized a long time ago. It's time to let them go.

When we focus on what we have not achieved, or how we are not living the life of our dreams, we exist in a state of lack.

We're focused on what we do not have instead of realizing gratitude for what we have accomplished and what we have been blessed with in our lives.

This is where our ego-mind gets in the way and keeps us locked in our comfort zone.

Even though we may not be happy with our life as it exists, it is familiar and comfortable in some ways. That's what makes it dangerous to our growth.

Comfort, like a frog in a slowly-warming pot of water, will lead to the death of our dreams.

If a live frog is placed into a pot of boiling water, the shock of the heat will cause him to reflexively jump out to safety.

But, if the frog is placed in a pot of cool water, and the heat is turned up slowly, he will acclimate to each new, warmer temperature.

Eventually, he dies from exposure to the excessive heat.

We do the same thing as we develop stages of comfort in our lives. Like the slowly warming water around the frog, we become oblivious to how the familiarity of our environment may be slowly killing us.

When we allow ourselves to take an objective look at our lives and address the underlying stress we're feeling, we might finally jump for our lives.

Familiarity and Fear of Success

When I work with clients who have an entrepreneurial goal, it is eye-opening for many of them to realize that the fear of success is far more powerful than the fear of failure.

If they fail, they can keep on being who they are: same familiar life, same familiar friends, same familiar struggles; but if they succeed, then their life changes.

In success, they may have to be a different person as they run their business, learn new skills, meet new friends and associates, and let go of the things that have held them back (which includes subconscious beliefs, material things and, quite possibly, negative family members and friends).

Those are scary thoughts. Ones that limit many, many people.

It is possible to overcome these fears and develop a new outlook. Hypnotherapy is one avenue, counseling and coaching are other modalities that can help. Either way, one key to success is to have a positive supporter/mentor/coach/counselor guiding you on your path to change.

As humans, we're wired to see what's different. We tend to compare ourselves to others who we admire. When we do, we usually focus on where we fall short of these icons, rather than making a plan to aspire and achieve.

That's our ego getting in the way.

When we begin to refocus and reprogram our subconscious to see the good things that we have in our life, then we move to a foundation of gratitude and begin to open the doors to the Divine Will guiding us.

I've previously mentioned that your dreams do not come from a vacuum. God, The Source, The Universe, The Divine, or whatever name is comfortable for you does not toy with us. It does not present ideas of achievement to us as though they were carrots dangling before a horse.

We can achieve every goal, every dream, in our mind when we realize that it is being given to us from a supportive source that wants us to succeed.

The Universe is The Source of All things. The ultimate results are available to us to make this physical realm the best it can be.

You are not apart from the Universe,
you are A Part of the Universe.

Our ego-mind keeps us small in the safety of the familiar. Not because it's trying to harm us; it just doesn't know any better. It is stuck in its comfort zone.

In its way, our ego is protecting us from the hurt of failure, the hurt of success, or maybe of just being hurt period.

It is working from fear.

The Universe is the energy of love which is a much more powerful emotion because it vibrates at the highest level that we can possibly achieve.

Let's get to work.

Gratitude is our expression of love back to the Universe.

By realizing and acknowledging the things which bless our lives, we are letting the Universe know that we are paying attention to it and saying, "Thank You."

One of the most important assignments I give to my clients is to perform gratitude exercises.

Mainly, I suggest that they purchase a copy of *The Five-Minute Journal* by Intelligent Change and begin filling it out immediately.

These exercises also play an important role in re-aligning our Reticular Activating System (RAS) to perceive the good things in our lives, instead of constantly focusing our shortcomings.

As our awareness of the good that is present in our lives grows, we begin to sense the abundance of positive energy in our surroundings and see that we are deserving and worthy of more good things.

Remember to look from gratitude, not from lack.

How do you receive your allowance from The Universe?

Let's consider what gratitude looks like in terms of how we receive our gifts from The Universe.

Let's examine a familiar scenario. Imagine a parent has chosen to give an allowance to his/her child. They want the child to understand money and begin having a healthy relationship with finances.

When they give the child five dollars, the child responds, "That's not enough. Billy's mom gives him twenty dollars! I want more!"

How do you think the parent feels in this moment? What thoughts may be running through their head? Maybe, "Well, if you don't appreciate what I have to give you now, I won't give you anything," or "Until you show me you can be responsible with a small amount of money, I'm not going to give you more."

Does this story remind you of how you may be talking to The Universe when your goal is not delivered to you in *exactly the way you want it to be?*

What may have been the outcome if the child had said, "Thank you" for the five-dollar gift?

By showing gratitude for what exists as the present gift, the child opens up an opportunity to receive more when his/her parent decides that s/he has become responsible enough to receive more money.

When we graciously receive gifts from The Universe that may be smaller than our desired outcome, we are sending back a message of appreciation.

If you don't feel like those small outcomes are good enough to get you where you want to go within your desired timeframe, then you need to look at re-tooling your actions or re-evaluating your deadline.

Examining your progress at this time must come from a place of gratitude for your accomplishments.

If you are having a difficult time quieting the negative feelings or voices that you have about your progress, please realize that this is just your ego distracting you with false, learned beliefs.

Rather than listening to and falling prey to those negative perceptions, take a moment to stop, breathe and think.

We'll take action shortly.

For now, it's time to just stop for a moment and become an observer of your actions. No judgment, no emotion, just objective observation.

Why? Because we need to examine if the actions that you have been taking are actually moving you toward your goal.

What if they were actually moving you away from your objective or, worse yet, not moving you anywhere productive at all?

As we progress through the next few steps, keep in mind that this exercise is intended to come from a place of gratitude.

Reinforce what you have completed – that's where you will build your strength to keep going.

Action Step #1: Write down your accomplishments.

Make a list of every single achievement, no matter how large or small, that has brought you closer to your goal.

If you were to draw a map of your progress, how far would you be along your path to accomplishment?

START --- GOAL

It is important for you to fully realize at this moment that there are no failures. There are only faulty timeframes.

If you have not accomplished your outcome, evaluate your progress and set a new date for achievement. Congratulations on moving ahead. Your path to achievement is now shorter, your goal is closer than it was when you began this program.

Action Step #2: Stop and Breathe

When you feel fear or apprehension creeping in, follow these three actions:

1. Stop.

2. Meditate.

3. Listen to your Higher Consciousness.

Take a deep breath, relax and take intentional action.

Ask your fear why it is there.

If it won't answer, ask your Higher Consciousness for insight.

The answer to this question is key in understanding how a part of your subconscious is trying to help you by holding you back.

Once you understand the motivations for the fear, gently thank them and let them know that they no longer have a place in your life. It's time for them to change their job and help you move forward to achieve your Highest Purpose.

Iris' Insights

Divine Will is truth, wisdom and spiritual insight which can help us awaken and maintain a healthy well-being in our daily lives through the acceptance of what is. It is when the human will is surrendered and one knows the Divine Will and that all that matters is that "it is the way things are." In Hinduism this is considered to be the principle of cosmic order.

To live in "grace" is to be free of ego conditioning and to understand the ultimate truth - that we do not choose. Yet the relative truth is that we do make choices. It is hard for the mind to hold these two opposite truths, but they do not oppose each other. The ultimate truth is that everything unfolds according to Divine Will, yet choices of ego-conditioned individuals do exist and "interfere" with Divine Will, but only for a short while as the Law of Adjustment kicks in. (More on that later.) If we cooperate with Divine Will and possibly also experience it more fully, we can realize our choice is to follow Divine Will.

Meditation to Connect with Divine Will

Prepare to sit in meditation. Focus on your breathing and relax the body as your breath goes in and out. Start at your feet and work your way up to the top of your head until your entire body is relaxed. Focus on your breath and feel as if you are breathing into the center of your chest next to the heart.

You are in search of a still-point within you. It is an empty space; time is suspended there. You may see a brilliant white light or sense a presence there. This is the essence of your Divine Self/True Self/Soul. Be one with this essence. Open up to your Divine Self. It is love, peace, unity, bliss, power and higher wisdom knowledge.

Allow the distractions of the physical world to dissolve or float away. Restore yourself in the light and feel the love and power of this Self and be one with It. Become It. It will reveal the illusions, desires, and attachments that keep you trapped in a lower vibration which you need to release.

The Divine Self knows all. Ask for guidance, insight, or an answer to a question you may have as you sit in silence. Be receptive. Know and trust that you are aligned with your divinity and that guidance will happen in some way, at some time. It may be immediate or it may not.

Stay in the still-point for as long as you can, staying connected to this Divine Essence. You may receive an inner message which may come through a sense of energy, deeper peace, an inner knowing, an unspoken answer or in other ways during and after this meditation.

Then take a deep breath or two in and out and open your eyes when you are ready.

Be patient, open, and aware while the answers and guidance unfold and then follow it.

13: The Law of Dharma

What is the single most important step to being happy?

Through the Law of Will, you learned how to get out of your own way by realizing that by aligning your ego-mind with Divine Will, you will receive what you wanted anyway.

That leads us to the concept of Dharma.

Your Dharma is your life purpose. It is what you, and you alone, are here to do on this planet in this lifetime.

Earlier in this book, I suggested that you should have big goals, goals that are in service to others and make the world a better place. You are a unique individual and there is *something that only you can do* on this Earth. That is your Dharma.

By realizing this purpose, you will be living in alignment with your innate skills and interests. You will, therefore, live a happier life.

I'm not saying it will be easier. There will be challenges, you can count on that, and you will have to take action. But you will experience a happier life when you are living in alignment with your passions.

Rather than grinding your life away at a job that merely provides you a paycheck every week or two, waiting for retirement, you will be able to wake up every day excited for what lies ahead of you.

In his book, *The Blue Zones,* Dan Buettner described an interesting language phenomenon in Okinawa, Japan.

The people of Okinawa do not have a word in their language for retirement. Instead, they have the word, *ikigai* which roughly means "that which makes one's life worth living," according to National Geographic.

This is living with purpose, waking every day to excitement about the present moment, eager to encounter the day.

Isaiah Hankel also described this idea in his life-changing book, *Black Hole Focus*.

Yet, is this how most of us live?

Sadly, the answer is no.

We dread waking up in the morning because we know we're just going to work or some other obligation. We're excited for weekends, vacations and, far off in the distance, that mysterious, mythical tropical island known as "Retirement."

Living this way, we are wasting our talents and our lives.

Waking with these negative feelings only increases our resistance to manifesting our desired, happy life.

This is why so many people think the Law of Attraction does not work for them. They wish for something better but maintain the emotional outlook of their present discord.

Discovering your purpose may just be the single most important step in manifesting your ideal life.

How do you discover your purpose?

Well, take some time to focus on what brings you happiness. What things interest you and fulfill you?

Ask yourself, "Why am I going to work today?" The first response you may hear might be, "Because I need to earn money to support myself and my family. But there is more to it than just that. There is a reason that you are going to *this particular* job. Listen for the deeper answer.

Do you enjoy painting, exercising, teaching, helping others, or building things?

The question now becomes, why aren't you doing these activities every day? How can you turn your purpose into the work that you do and be paid for it?

Ego-mind would have us strive for a paycheck and an illusion of security. Instead of following your dream to become an artist or historian, you instead take a job in computers or accounting because, "That's where the money is."

Then you go to work each morning dreading the boring and tedious nature of your existence in a job that lacks creative expression. On the weekends, once you recover from the negativity that you surround yourself with for five days, you come alive as you engage with your hobbies, fulfilling yourself and bringing joy to others.

Then Monday comes. Again. And again. And again.

This type of life is a death spiral. (Yes, technically, by default, life in general is a death spiral, but here's a news flash: YOU ARE ALLOWED TO ENJOY THE RIDE!)

Prior to becoming a hypnotherapist, I was working in a job that was draining my soul.

After discovering the concept of *ikigai,* I began asking myself, every day, why I was going to this job that was no longer fulfilling. I knew the answer was larger than just going for the paycheck, which was good.

I knew there was something larger, an answer which spoke to my soul.

It took three weeks of daily questioning for the answer to present itself.

In that moment, I realized that I had a passion for problem-solving and for helping others to live better, happier lives. From that moment, I began choosing to live my life to fulfill that purpose rather than to chase a paycheck.

When you have an idea of what your purpose may be, meditate on it.

Remove all of the distractions that surround you: social media, television, radio, other people, etc. Take some time to quietly focus on YOU.

It's natural for us to want to be part of a group, to feel included and share experiences. However, when these actions keep us from taking care of ourselves first, we lose track of who we are and what we're supposed to be doing.

We start living to fulfill how others see us instead of living to manifest our purpose.

You are not on this earth to give up your Dharma for the approval of others. Stop trying to fit in by lowering your expectations and hanging out with under-achievers.

I can hear you saying, "But that's not nice. That's selfish."

Yes, it is. And it's the healthiest thing you can do for yourself.

We're told from a young age that being selfish is bad, that we should share and focus on making others happy.

That's bullshit.

How can you expect to take care of others if you (1) don't know your purpose, and (2) don't take care of yourself to have the strength to help others?

I like to call this the "airplane oxygen mask metaphor." You are useless to others if you pass out first and can't take care of yourself. Secure your mask before helping those around you;

114

otherwise, you will diminish resources there to help those who can't help themselves.

And, there is no guarantee that those other people will help you once they get their masks secured. You must take care of yourself first.

It's time to get focused.

In the era of social media, we're more connected as a species than ever before in history. Yet, how do we use this amazing tool?

We post selfies, share images of our meals, shoot videos at concerts, and give away too much information on a regular basis. Oh, and we promote videos of cats...

How is this helping us discover our Dharma?

It's not. It is a distraction created by our ego to feed our ego.

Using technology in this way is nothing more than an advanced way of saying, "Look at me!! Look at what I can do," like an attention-starved child standing on a diving board trying to catch his parents' attention.

Instead of sharing our true talents, many of us post videos of ourselves doing something foolish...because self-deprecation always garners a ton of likes. Seeing these "thumbs-up" symbols triggers dopamine to be released in our brains and we become slowly addicted to repeating the process as we drunkenly feed our ego more junk food.

Social media is a drug keeping you from actualization of your higher purpose. It's time to stop. As Nancy Reagan would say, *"Just Say NO."*

(Oh, and yes, social media, just like drugs and other tools, does have a useful place in helping us improve our lives. It must be applied with awareness as to why we are using it, instead of allowing it to be a mere distraction from our boring existence.)

In this moment, it is time for you to declare a war on distraction.

To paraphrase Elmer Fudd: *We're hunting for Dharma. It's Dharma Season.*

EXERCISES

1. List the things that bring you happiness.

What activities do you enjoy doing? What things are you really good at, better than anyone else you know?

What do others appreciate you doing for them that you also enjoy doing? (To be honest, taking the trash out for your spouse may or may not apply...)

Make a list of these activities. It does not have to be too detailed, just enough information for you to recall and reconnect with.

2. Focus on each activity separately.

As you focus on each of your noted actions, take time to sense how you feel about them.

Does your heart race with excitement when you read your entry, or does your chest feel heavy with dread? Maybe you feel butterflies in your stomach, good ones that tell you that you're on a path of growth and positive challenges.

Take time to sense the feelings that accompany your notes.

Do not rush this process. Be slow and deliberate. This is key.

Cross off those items that bring you a sense of unease.

Highlight the items that bring you a sense of happiness, joy and excitement.

3. Meditate on the highlighted notes.

Find a place to sit quietly where you will not be distracted.

Turn off your phone. Turn off the radio. Place a "Do not disturb" sign on the door. Turn off the TV. Just unplug.

Disconnect from the world for 30 minutes. Give yourself permission to do this.

Relax. The world will still be there when you come back.

Look at your sheet of highlighted notes. Pick one item – the one that brings you the most excitement.

Commit it to memory, close your eyes and take a deep breath.

As you exhale, focus your mind on that activity and, more importantly, on the good feelings associated with it.

Ask for imagery showing how your life would look if you were living it with this as your purpose and focus. How would your life be different than it is now? How would you feel? Do you desire this to be your life? If the answer is yes, then what steps do you need to take to begin manifesting this as your reality?

When your meditation time is complete, add the answer to these questions to your notes. As you write, what one thing stands out to you as the first item you are excited to do?

Go do it. NOW.

Iris' Insights

Meditation to Find Your Purpose

As we discussed previously regarding The Law of Will, Divine Will (Dharma) is truth, wisdom and spiritual insight. It is "the way things are." Here you will discover your personal Dharma, which normally coincides with The Dharma of Divine Will.

Repeat the meditation to connect with Divine Will. When you are able to stay in the still-point and all distractions of emotions and thoughts and senses are released, then ask, "How can I be of service to the Divine?" "What is the reason for this existence?" "What does my path entail?" "What do I need to do?" The answers to these questions and more will allow you to find your purpose and accomplish what you have come to do in this lifetime.

Ask that you be shown in your day-to-day life, through signs, synchronicities, etc., Divine Will's guidance that brings you those people and situations that will help you to find and fulfill your purpose. Stay in the still-point for as long as you can and remain connected to the Divine Essence within you.

Then take a deep breath or two in and out and open your eyes when you are ready.

Again, be patient, open and aware while the answers and guidance unfold.

14: The Law of Adjustment

Why are you choosing to be unhappy?

Recently, I read Mo Gawdat's amazing book, *Solve for Happy.*

I first became aware of Mr. Gawdat, the former Chief Business Officer for Google [X], through a video on Facebook in which he discusses the basic concepts of his algorithm for happiness.

It's a pretty simple process, really. As Mr. Gawdat writes, happiness is the default state of human beings. In his observation (and the observations of others), children are naturally happy. They find joy and pleasure in the world until the moment when they begin to internalize perceptions that something is wrong.

At that time, there is a disconnect with their existing situation and their intended situation. They learn to be unhappy. They, actually we, begin to see life from a perception of lack instead of one of flow, balance, and connection.

From this perspective, we are viewing our position in life from an ego-centric outlook that defines our value and worth through external symbols: Our job title, the cost of our home, the model of our car, and the size of our bank account, for example.

These factors are not us; they are merely symbols. When we become enmeshed in viewing our value in this way, we disconnect from our purpose and connect to temporary things.

When those things eventually change, as all temporary things do, then we begin to feel loss associated with the degree of self that we have invested in those items.

In Western culture, we have an ingrained sense that we must always be moving forward and improving these external factors. Particularly in America, we're programmed to be achievers. Hard work wins the day, or so we're told.

We can't stop to breathe or to find a moment of peace and clarity, because we've been told that if we stop, then someone will overtake us. They will reach our achievement before us.

Let's break down why that's just stupid thinking.

The Law of Dharma says that you have a unique purpose here on this planet in this lifetime.

If you agree that you have a purpose here, an outcome that only you can achieve because of your singular experience of life – from your childhood to the present moment – then it is faulty logic to think that someone else will achieve it before (or instead) of you.

They are not you. And, conversely, you are not them.

Sure, someone may do something similar, but they are not expressing YOUR vision, YOUR Dharma. They are expressing theirs.

Feeling discouraged when you see someone else seemingly presenting your ideas is understandable, but where is this feeling of frustration rooted?

It is rooted in ego. It is not coming from your Higher Self.

Our disharmony always comes from ego. We learn to be dissatisfied with life rather than embracing a perception of balance, peace, and happiness that is our natural state of being.

I love the metaphor that Mr. Gawdat uses to describe our journey from childhood happiness and alignment to adulthood stress. In his terms, we are like a smartphone: we come with a default setting for happiness, just as a smart device comes from the factory with default settings that the engineers feel are optimum for performance of the device.

As we add apps to our device, or change the settings, we are also altering the performance of the instrument. Sometimes these additions are detrimental to its optimal performance.

In our life, we take on faulty beliefs that separate us from our default state of happiness. We feel hurt, we feel disappointed, we perceive loss…all of which are events, yet instead of viewing them as just events, we deliver larger meaning to them. Like the imaginary siblings we discussed earlier, we connect with these beliefs and ascribe emotional meaning to them.

Those emotional connections make it harder to break free from this old thinking.

One of the biggest barriers we create for ourselves is when we view events as endpoints instead of as markers on our journey.

We tell ourselves stories of why these events occurred. These stories tend to reinforce a limiting belief structure that keeps us out of alignment.

An example of this type of faulty thinking is showcased in the phrase, "waiting for the other shoe to drop." In other words, living in a state of dread that something bad is going to happen, or that because something good just happened (a raise, a new job, a new relationship…), a balancing or reckoning must be right around the corner.

Why? Because, well, life can't be all good, can it?

You are correct. Life will not always seem to be all good. There will always be challenges.

However, we must decide whether we are the victims of challenges, or observers of them.

We are beings of free will. We can choose how we perceive events; we choose the stories that we apply to the things that happen around us.

How can we make this shift in thinking?

Lesson 1: There Is No Other Shoe

You've probably lived your life weighing good events against bad ones.

This is a learned habit that your ego internalized. It is only a story, one perception of a series of events. It is not true.

In this mode of life, you are nothing more than a teeter-totter shifting helplessly as outside forces tip you left and right. Always seeking balance, you apply perceptional weight to the opposing force.

Maybe you just received an unexpected check for your birthday last week. Let's say it's $50.

Huh, the gas bill came due today and it's $52 higher than normal. Bummer, there goes that windfall.

Received a big (and I mean BIG) promotion at work, bonus included? Uh oh, the water pump in your car just broke…oh, and due to poor engineering on the part of the manufacturer, it took your entire engine out at the same time. Say goodbye to $5,000 for a new one.

Never going to get ahead, right? The Universe is against your success, right?

No. It is not.

In each of these illustrations, the negative event that occurred after the positive one HAS NOTHING TO DO WITH THE POSITIVE EVENT.

They are two entirely separate occurrences. It is only in our mind, from our ego-driven perspective, that they have any connection.

There is no "other shoe." There are only events. How we define them affects our outlook and happiness.

If you are unwilling to give up the idea that the events are connected, could you view these occurrences differently?

Absolutely. Here's how:

Let's use the car example. Remove your promotion from the equation. In this scenario, you are still doing the same job, for the same pay.

Oooops...your car just broke down. Dead engine. Do not pass Go, pay $5,000.

Where will this money come from if you did not get the promotion? How do you feel?

PERSPECTIVE SHIFT: The unexpected bill did not come as punishment because you moved ahead. The positive event occurred so that you could financially navigate the impending problem.

The Universe has your back.

Do you feel happier knowing that the money came to help you, rather than the bill coming to punish you?

Let go of the stories of lack that come from your ego and connect back with the higher awareness that comes from aligning with your default state of happiness.

You have the power to choose to define your life differently. Be a victim or be a victor – the choice is yours.

Choose the story that connects events in a way that empowers you. The events exist anyway. You create the connection between them. Make it a good one.

Lesson #2: You Get More Of What You Focus On

As I look at the Amazon reviews for Mr. Gawdat's book, I am struck by the 5% of reviewers (as of this writing) who give the book only two stars. I'm curious about their perceptions in contrast to the 85% who promote the book as 5-star.

One sentence stood out to me in one of these reviews.

"It basically comes down to how to manage your expectations of life. Obviously, he has achieved an impressive sense of personal calm, but that doesn't mean that he can teach it."

And there it is.

It appears that this reviewer understood the message of the book, but it seems that he did not want to accept it.

Instead of turning inward to ask himself why he feels this way, he chooses to publicly display his frustration by inferring that Mr. Gawdat cannot teach the subject because this reviewer did not create a shift in his personal thinking.

That's ego talking.

I don't know this person, nor do I have any personal stake in the outcome of his life.

What I do know is that as long as he is in the process of searching for happiness/personal improvement (evident by his purchase of this book) and he is unwilling to accept a new perception of events, then he will not move forward.

As a free-willed human being, that's his choice. I bless him and wish him well on his journey.

When we're searching for answers, it's very easy (frighteningly so) to stay stuck in our old story. That's more ego-stuff keeping us in a not-so-comfortable comfort zone.

Why are there so many self-help books? Because most of us need help – we have a vision of something better for our lives, but that is not the life we are living. Hence, we feel discord, stress and frustration.

Why isn't there just one grand "go-to" self-help authority? Because we are all different and, while we are looking for answers within the same space, we each respond to different messaging. Some ideas that we embrace, others will discard; some ideas that other's find helpful, we think are bullshit.

Why won't something new work? The answer comes back, "Because nothing has worked before. Why should I trust this? Sounds like the same thing I've heard a million times before."

That voice is a protective mechanism. It's trying to help you by steering you away from the pain of disappointment. Unfortunately, it can also make you stop short of achieving your goal.

How many swings of a hammer does it take to break a brick wall? Maybe one person can do it in 5, maybe someone else will need 20…Maybe you'll need 101.

Looking back, how would you feel if you found out that you stopped your journey with swing 100?

Maybe you were tired at that moment when you quit. Maybe you were bored or frustrated because you were finding just more brick behind the blocks that you had already chipped away.

Or, maybe it's because you heard an inner voice saying, "This is useless."

That voice did not want you to break through the wall. It wanted you to stay in your comfort zone.

Let's take that next swing by changing our perception.

PERCEPTION SHIFT: The Law of Adjustment states that there is a harmony to the Universe. I am, and you are, part of that harmony. Happiness, harmony, and flow are our natural state.

If you cringed at that sentence, please follow this syllogism:

The Universe is harmony,
I am part of the Universe,
Therefore, I am part of harmony.

Now, get over your ego and accept that statement.

You are here on this earth for a purpose. No one else can do it. They may produce something similar, but YOU are here for YOUR unique addition to the *body of literature* known as human experience.

You are a note in the harmony. Without your participation, the song will not sound the same.

When we accept that our lives have a purpose in something larger, it becomes easier to accept that perceived negative situations actually have a role in our growth. They are lessons.

When we fight the lesson, we are out of adjustment with our Higher Purpose. We're struggling in ego-land saying things like, "It shouldn't be this hard," or "Ugh. I'll never get ahead."

When we become aware that we are out of alignment with the Universe, then it is time for us to surrender to what exists, choose to stop struggling and allow our life to come back into adjustment with our purpose.

What does life look like when we choose to live in alignment with our goals and allow happiness to be our default state of being?

We become like one of my favorite characters, Pete the Cat.

Pete came into artist James Dean's life and then nudged his way into Dean's art. In recent years, Dean has begun producing children's books featuring this wonderful cat.

My favorite is, *I Love My White Shoes.*

What is it about this particular book that I love so much? I love that Pete's attitude to life is unassailable. He has invincible confidence that cannot be diminished by seemingly unfortunate events.

In this book, James Dean uses Pete to show kids that life does not have to be a series of disappointments due to external events.

As Pete's white shoes change colors due to a variety of mishaps, Pete loves each new hue as much as the previous one. He continues singing his song, changing only the name of the color as he dances down the street.

For Pete, all is well, no matter what. His life is flow. Each state is perfect as he experiences his life. In every moment, he knows that he is exactly where he is supposed to be and accepts that situation with grace and peace.

Yet, there are still those who do not understand this message. They illustrate resistance to flow.

Here's a snippet from one of the Amazon reviews:

> *"Bright, childlike illustrations show the long-limbed feline regularly altering his footwear but continuing not to watch where he's walking. The moral of the story keep going no matter what happens to you in life may sound like good advice, but it doesn't instill any sense of power in children it just tells them to accept their fate."*

While it is practical advice that one should watch where one is walking, sometimes obstacles are unavoidable.

This illustrated book is not about the acceptance of fate. It is about choosing not to frame temporary situations as losses that make one a victim of external events.

What will you do when the metaphorical shoes that are your life turn red, or blue, yellow, or just get dirty from experience? Will you lament that you no longer have white shoes, or will you choose the power of accepting your new reality and adjust accordingly?

Pete, like Mr. Gawdat, recognizes his situation and chooses how he will respond to it. He chooses happiness.

Living this way is about being so in tune with yourself that nothing outside of you can harm your perception of your strength and happiness.

That's instilling real power in children (of all ages).

EXERCISES

1. Defining the Obstacle

What is the biggest challenge you see in your life today? What obstacle do you struggle to overcome?

Take time now to look beyond it. Become an observer of it and realize that it is your current state of being.

What thoughts do you have about this state of disharmony? What negative perceptions are you carrying?

Write all of these negative ideas down on a sheet of paper. Fold it over, seal it tight. Make it so secure that it's as if these ideas can't escape.

On the outside of the packet that you just created, write the answer to this question:

"What do I need to do to overcome these feelings/perceptions? How do I minimize their influence on my life?"

From this moment forward, when these frustrations come to mind, remember this piece of paper. You merely need to connect with that solution to reduce or remove the obstacle.

2. Magic Wand

What are the thoughts you would like to have about your intended outcome?

How would you feel if you waved a magic wand and *WHOOSH* your dream was suddenly your reality? How would your life be different in this new environment? What would you do with your money/time/life?

Take a deep breath, close your eyes and mediate on these positive thoughts and feelings. Bring them into the present moment and replace the old negative thoughts with these new ideas.

Do this every day. Live your life, express yourself, as though this vision is your life right now.

Iris' Insights

We must accept that God/Divine Will is the only power. All is under the authority of God for It is the Creator. Whatever is out of order or contradictory can have no basic standard of its own. Ego can do nothing to increase, stop, or intensify the action of The Creator.

We must surrender our ego conditioned thoughts and emotions and realize that all that is conceptualized, felt, seen, and heard and tasted is part of a dream. True reality is beneath the dream. Divine Energy and Consciousness always flows through, untarnished. What is supposed to be is consistently in step with The Flow of The Universe, adjusting and moving around ego projections. We must establish that we are part of this Flow and be It through the surrender of all that we are not. You are the "U" in Universe.

Meditation on The Universal Flow

Prepare to sit in meditation and take a couple of deep breaths in and out. Breathe deeply focusing on your breathing. Relax the body starting at your feet moving to the top of your head.

Now visualize above your head a magnificent radiant golden white sun. This is The Great Central Sun of Source/Creator. See and/or feel the amazing rays of light filled with pure energy of Source/Creator flowing through your crown, filling your entire body as it flows down the vertical core along your spine and out through the soles of your feet. Feel the rejuvenating vitality of the life force within the pure energy.

Now sense the power of creation within the pure energy. Sense that God Consciousness, the pure consciousness, is manifesting what is supposed to be through this energy. Sense the stream of the Universal Flow as a perfectly balanced and blended wave of energy and consciousness ever creating, unaffected by any ego dreams.

Sense that you are part of this Flow for if all else is a dream and you are conscious, you must be the pure consciousness that is one with pure energy within the most luminous light of Source. Be that which you are. Allow all else to fall away. Just be.

Open your eyes when you are ready and ground yourself by feeling that you are in the body. Remember you are The Flow within it. Continue to identify with The Flow for as long are you are able as you go about your day.

15: The Law of Polarity

Why what you don't want is really what you want.

Heads or tails? Hot or cold? Front or back? Left or right? Day or night? Yin or Yang? Happy or sad?

When we begin the journey to change our life, we initially view our situation as one of have/have not.

There is what we "have" present in our life, typically a situation that is creating stress.

Then there is what we "have not." Usually, these missing elements include peace, calm, relaxation, financial freedom, and a sense of balance.

If this seems counter-intuitive to you, congratulations. You are realizing that we humans tend to live our lives out of alignment, striving for short-term relief (or validating false stories from our ego), instead of focusing on our long-term goals.

We choose to pursue a regular, steady paycheck at a job that is not fulfilling rather than doing work for which we have passion. When we actually do choose to take action on our passions so that we have some sense of joy, we tend to relegate these activities to mere hobbies instead of a lifestyle.

In the previous chapter, as part of our discussion on the Law of Adjustment, I offered the idea that mankind is naturally wired to be happy as our default state of being.

Why then do we allow ourselves to be mired in unhappiness?

One possible explanation is negativity bias.

Negativity is a tool for survival. It has kept humans alive for thousands of years.

Unfortunately, we get stuck in this mode, filling our Reticular Activating System (RAS) with fear, anger, and disempowering ideas regarding our sense of worth.

In this mode, we focus on obstacles instead of opportunities.

Newsflash: Obstacles are opportunities.

Moving from the negative environment that is present, we may tend to think of our goal as a separate existence. It feels so far removed from where we are, that it's almost inconceivable to think that we could achieve this new outcome. That's an understandable point-of-view.

If your perspective is coming from being poor, the concept of rich seems like it could only take place in another life, or for another person. Where is your frame of reference for financial abundance when you are struggling with debt or just getting by?

This perspective is a trap on many levels.

Not only does it tie us vibrationally to the low-level discharge of poor (which resonates out to the Universe and attracts more poor-ness to us, thanks to the Law of Attraction), it also separates us from our potential.

The negative power of "or."

This sense of duality, invoking the word "or," also interrupts our connection to the Flow by interrupting the Law of Polarity.

We think we are either "rich" or "poor," "healthy" or "sick," when in fact we are each of those things at the same time.

The Law of Polarity recognizes that all things are included in their opposites. What appear to be separate concepts are actually degrees of the same idea and they exist in a state of flow.

Visually, the Law of Polarity is illustrated by the Tao symbol of Yin/Yang. Each element contains its opposite and these forces exist equally and simultaneously.

When does day become night? When does light become dark? Is there not a degree of light within the darkness of night, just as there is shadow during the day?

At what point does the head side of a coin become tails? Are they not the same coin? If we flip the coin and it lands heads-up, does the tail side cease to exist?

Understanding polarity and flow

When does your current life become your new life? In one massive shift, or in a series of minor adjustments?

When you are angry, at what point do you become happy?

When you are neither happy nor angry, what are you?

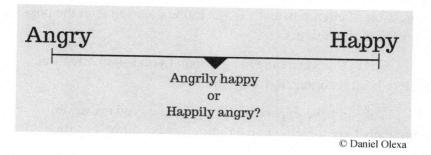

© Daniel Olexa

If we view anger and happiness as a linear scale, with each emotion represented at the extremes, at what point does anger become happiness?

While treated as separate emotional states, the feelings known as "angry" and "happy" are merely opposite expressions of a single emotional range. They are conjoined terms, existing as an inseparable pair.

Without happy, we could not know the frustration that comes when we are out of alignment and experiencing anger. In this case, anger is our warning sign that we are not experiencing happiness.

Without anger, we could not appreciate happy.

When we're not stuck in one state or the other, when we allow ourselves to become observers of our emotions, we see that our emotions flow naturally.

Anger does not immediately give way to happiness. It slowly evolves along the continuum from anger to frustration to sadness to acceptance to peace to happy.

There are no good or bad emotions; however there may be negative expressions of those emotions. That's ego acting out, not emotion.

Ego tells us that we're justified in overly expressing ourselves, that we deserve to get attention. Sadly, the negative expression of emotions tends to get more attention than the positive expression of emotions.

And yes, even someone glaring at you is still attention. You've been recognized. Congratulations.

As you have experienced in your life, you are never completely experiencing one emotion permanently. Emotions flow.

Unfortunately, because of our negativity bias, we tend to get stuck focusing on the emotions that resonate with frustration. This level of attention leads us to view the happy moments as seemingly all too fleeting, while our darker times feel like they are ever-present.

How does The Law of Polarity apply to your situation in life?

The current state of being that you wish to change is merely a reflection of the state that you desire to achieve.

You are probably, at this moment, in a state of "have not," feeling stressed or frustrated because you are eager for a state where you "have" peace, happiness, abundance, etc.

Sometimes, it seems as if our goal exists as a completely separate life from our current situation.

Both states exist in the framework of your life. If you think about your life, you have probably experienced times which matched your ideal outcome. At these times, you felt powerful, happy and in balance with your goals.

In fact, there are probably elements of your outcome that exist in your life right now, but you aren't aware of them because you are fixating your attention on the obstacles.

It's time to become aware of the right things.

Your emotional GPS

When you get in your car to take a trip to a new restaurant, you probably use a GPS to find out the most efficient path to the destination.

If your GPS did not have an accurate location for your starting point, you would not be given helpful directions to reach the restaurant.

Let's look at it this way: If you were in Los Angeles preparing to drive to Chicago, would it be helpful to you if your GPS thought you were starting from New York?

Probably not. Actually, not at all. If you drive west from Los Angeles, you'll just wind up cold, wet, and miserable as your car goes into the Pacific.

Unfortunately, that is exactly what we do when we try to create our outcomes: We do not take an accurate positioning of where we are in life at the moment we are beginning our journey.

This can be seen in statements like, "I wish I wouldn't have waited until I was 50 to do this. I should have done it at 30."

Or, "I wish I would have taken that other job ten years ago. I'd have money in the bank now."

The hard truth is you cannot change the past. Longingly wishing for something that didn't happen will not help you to move forward as you create your future.

It is critical at this point of your manifesting process to recognize where you are right at this moment.

EXERCISE: Be here now

If you are feeling stuck and frustrated, then stop, breathe and relax.

Get out of your way by removing your resistance to what is. Recognize that the state of "have not" is resulting in frustration. It is just part of the flow to your state of "have."

Acknowledging the present situation is not accepting and embracing it as though it is a permanent state.

Recognition of your current state is nothing more than declaring, "This is where I am right now."

Once you know where you are, you can move forward with efficiency.

When you examine your current life under the lens of the Law of Polarity, what elements of your desired life already exist that can support your achievement of your goal?

As you focus on these elements and impress them to your RAS, ask yourself, "How can I work with these factors to increase their presence and impact?"

What things currently exist that you need to jettison? What do you need to do to remove (or lessen) these influences that have been holding you back?

Iris' Insights

Everything is a continuum. Yin and Yang show the balancing flow of this continuum. We can see that if there is an up there must be a down, failure and success, good and bad and so on; it is a world of duality. However, these opposites have no absolutes. There is not one point where you can say where one starts and the other begins. It is a variance along a scale range. Example: there is not one point where you can say that cold stops and heat begins; it is all on the same. There are two poles or opposites, which point to the extremes of one thing.

Everything is Dual; everything has poles; everything has its pair of opposites; like and unlike are the same; opposites are identical in nature, but different in degree; extremes meet; all truths are but half-truths; all paradoxes may be reconciled. --The Kybalion.

An understanding of the Law will enable one to change one's own polarity to find balance, which in turn affects others and all things. Mastery of the Law of Polarity requires learning how to maintain balance, focus, and detachment from the distractions of the material world.

Meditation on the Balance - Yin and Yang

Prepare to sit in meditation and take a couple of deep breaths in and out. Breathe deeply focusing on your breathing. Relax the body starting at your feet moving to the top of your head.

Now visualize and/or sense above your head a magnificent, radiant golden white sun, full of light. It is an intense and powerful pure energy. This is the Sun of Source/Creator. See and/or feel the amazing rays of light filled with pure energy of the Divine Creator flow through your crown filling your entire body as it flows down the vertical core long the spine to the groin and then around to the tailbone. This is Yang energy. It is forward movement, courage, and strength. It is the power of the creating force and life itself.

See and/or feel this energy and light flow up along the spine to the throat area; then flowing downward out the right side of the body through the bottom of your right foot deep into the earth.

As Yang flows through you, it connects with Earth Energy, Yin. Yin is cool and damp. It is material energy. It relaxes you and stabilizes Yang's potent force. Yin is the energy of matter that forms the outer world.

See and/or feel Yin bubbling up through your left foot and leg like cool water as it moves through the groin into the belly button area of your abdomen. See and/or feel Yin become solid there, like ice. Yang flows through and melts Yin again as soon as it forms, so that Yin may flow up the vertical core into the heart chakra (in the center of your chest next to the physical heart). Yin and Yang meet there, mingling together. They are one energy; just two poles on the scale of energy. There are no opposites truly, only extremes with varying levels of vibrations of energy in-between.

Feel Yin and Yang become one flow or wave within you. Balancing you; centering you; grounding you; and aligning you to that which you are – pure energy. Be the flow.

When you are done, take a cleansing, deep breath or two in and out and open your eyes when you are ready.

16: The Law of Intention and Desire

How to take action to show the Universe that you are serious

Have you ever noticed that when you take action, things just seem to fall into place?

We've come a long way on this journey together. Ideally, in that time you have made intentional steps toward achieving your goals.

From the start of this book, my mantra has been, "Wishing alone will not make it work. You have to take action."

Not long ago, I was doubting my mojo. It seemed like the great solar eclipse of 2017 had left me feeling tired and unmotivated.

Rather than give all my personal power over to a celestial event, I kept moving forward…researching, writing articles, networking.

Granted, I was moving at a slower pace than what is normal for me, but I kept moving forward. I didn't stop and say to myself, "I feel like crap this week, so I'll just wait until this feeling passes to do anything worthwhile."

Instead, I focused my energy. I produced a PowerPoint slideshow for a class that I developed, and another for a presentation. I started writing this chapter along with another on a different topic, and I completed an assignment for some powerful, advanced hypnotherapy training.

All good stuff.

What was I telling the Universe as I was slugging along during that week?

I was saying, "I'm ready. I'm doing the work required to achieve my goal."

What are you doing to tell the Universe that you are ready?

It's very easy to feel stuck at any point. When things aren't going our way, or when events just don't seem to be happening fast enough for us, it's a natural response to feel as though we are struggling to achieve our outcomes.

We may even feel that the Universe is against us.

After all, why would it provide us with a dream and then keep us from it? Is it watching us and laughing?

The Universe is not characterized by a sense of humor, nor is it cruel.

It is we humans who are cruel to ourselves through our application of finite, typically negative, beliefs about ourselves. These limiting thoughts come from our ego.

The Universe provides and creates. Human beings apply meaning to what has been created.

Early in this book, I presented to you the Law of Pure Potentiality: You can manifest anything you can dream of.

Time does not exist beyond our own need to define events.

The Universe, being timeless, is beyond our human concept of time.

In fact, time limits us. Or rather, our perception of time limits us.

Not only do we make statements that focus on our mortality, "I only have so many years," "There's not enough time in the day," "I'm already ___ years old. I can't do _____ anymore;" we also create an egocentric outlook that demands that events happen on OUR schedule because that's what we want.

When things don't happen within our declared deadline, we tend to feel like failures. We focus on what didn't happen. Sometimes we even give up on our goal.

It is time to stop limiting yourself. Stop believing old stories of failures. These stories are false.

I love this quote by Paul Coelho:

"And, when you want something, all the universe conspires in helping you to achieve it."

If you're not on board with that sentiment just yet, let's take a look at where you may be right now.

I hear you: If the Universe is conspiring with you, why is it taking so long for your goal to become real?

There are two possible answers.

1. You're not ready to receive your goal yet and the Universe is helping you to prepare by presenting you with challenges so that you may become the person you need to be to achieve your goal successfully. A crucible, if you will.

You may think you are ready for your outcome, but what if you're not?

What key piece of information are you missing or what lesson have you not yet learned?

2. You're in your own way, resonating with lower level vibrations, believing old, subconscious stories that are not empowering you. You are operating in fear, not in success.

Where is your focus – on the current challenge or your future success?

141

If you are obsessing on the obstacles of the present, you are not directing your energies toward achievement. While it is necessary to be aware of challenges so that you may address them, it is not productive to focus all of your attention on them.

Remember, we get more of what we focus our attention on.

It's time to become an observer. Accept the current situation, realize it is a temporary challenge that you will overcome, and then decide which action will best move you forward.

Get some movement going…An object at rest tends to stay at rest, while an object in motion tends to stay in motion. That's Newton's First Law.

You can choose your direction.

Will you move forward toward frustration, spiraling downward, filling your RAS with messages of limitations; or will you shift your mindset, realize the opportunities you have around you and take bold action to move toward your goals?

Choosing to move forward will activate the Law of Intention and Desire and show the Universe that you are serious about achieving your dreams.

EXERCISES

Sit quietly and meditate. Let go of any and all negative associations toward your current events.

Ground yourself and clear your mind of chatter.

Declare your intention to achieve your goal. Ask the Universe to help you by providing clear insights, clear opportunities, and realization of any lessons that you require to move forward.

Give thanks for your current situation. While superficially frustrating, this challenge has opened your eyes to a new opportunity for growth and a better way to live. Without this awareness, you would continue spiraling without direction.

Thank the Universe for its help in achieving your outcome. Act as if it has already occurred.

Question: What is the first action you are going to take as you declare your intention to the Universe?

Iris' Insights

The Law of Intention and Desire states that if you intend to manifest something and really want
to, then the Universe will support you. If you can dream it, so too can you manifest it. There are no unrealistic goals, only unrealistic time frames. Remember, however, that manifestation should only come from what The Divine Will "desires" and should be based only on your highest intentions.

EXERCISES

Ask yourself these questions daily and reflect upon the answers you receive:

Is this aligned with my higher values and way of life?

Does my intention and desire possibly fulfill what I came to do for the greater good of The All? Or, is it all based on ego gratification and self-importance?

Have I accepted all that is?

I am learning from my challenges?

Are things flowing in my life?

Am I being patient?

Am I trying to control?

You may discover more questions as you do this exercise which may help you to clearly define your higher intentions and know the Divine Will's resolve.

A Pessimist's Guide to Manifesting

17: The Law of Vibration

How Quantum Physics Supports the Law of Attraction

Periodically in this book, I have mentioned Newtonian Physics as a way of grounding the spiritual concept of manifesting in the three-dimensional, "real" world. Now it's time to play with Quantum Physics.

The three-dimensional world does not exist, at least not in the way our senses tell us it does.

You're probably reading his chapter while sitting down. How solid is that chair underneath you?

It feels very solid, right? Solid enough that you trust it to hold your weight.

How about the floor under it, the surface that is supporting the combined weight of both you and the chair? Seems solid…it certainly hurts if you accidentally trip, fall and impact against it.

What if I told you that these things, the chair and the floor, actually everything you see around you, is made up of mostly nothing?

Jonathan Bergmann provides a wonderful explanation of this in his animated TEDtalk.[1]

Go watch it.

Do it. It's only 5 minutes long.

Pretty amazing stuff, right?

What's the big takeaway?

Solid objects are mostly made of nothing. They are vast empty space.

Well, vast empty space that contains some electromagnetic energy.

What does electromagnetic energy do?

It vibrates.

Here's where Newtonian Physics is helpful in understanding the relationship of how vibrations respond to each other.

In his article for PBS,[2] Don Lincoln explains how subatomic particles interact. He uses this metaphor: "This is like having two people in boats and having one of them throw a sack to the other—the thrower's boat moves in response to the mass of the sack, as does the catcher's boat."

What are our thoughts? Energy.

What is most of our seemingly physical world made of? Energy.

What does energy do? It vibrates.

It is important at this point that we do not confuse magnetic energy with energy.

When looking at magnets, like charges repel each other. It is opposite charges that attract.

I prefer the energetic metaphor of a radio or television station. When your tuner is set to the right frequency, you receive the broadcast of that station.

Or, more accurately, in manifesting, you are the broadcast station and the Universe is the tuner.

What frequency are you sending out to the Universe? What signal is it listening to from you?

As your sending energy interacts with the Universe, the flow of vibrations returning to you is a reflection of your original output.

Are you hearing the music that you are wanting?

If not, it's time to change your tune.

EXERCISE

Become mindful of the signals you are receiving. What kind of radio station are you listening to?

Are you experiencing a life of upbeat happiness, peace and prosperity?

Or, does life feel like a classic country music song full of sorrow, drinkin', and lost dogs?

If you are not enjoying your station, it's time to change it. Realizing what you are listening to is the first step.

If you are perceiving the "same old, same old," it's time to change your out-going frequency.

Take action and change your vibrations. Begin feeling in-synch with positive intentions and actions that are in in alignment with your ideal outcome.

Iris' Insights

Science has shown that everything is energy - you, me... all things. All things have their own frequencies of vibration. We are bound by The Law of Vibration. This serves as the foundation for the Law of Attraction, as we can only accept similar or very close vibrational frequencies from "out there". If someone or something vibrates too high or too low, the energy is repelled.

Different frequencies of energy and consciousness within create our "bodies" or auras. Emotional energy vibrates a bit higher than dense physical energy, mental energy vibrates a bit higher than emotional energy. We must align with the highest frequencies we can as this brings better mental, emotional and physical health and sharper intellect, intuition and abilities. Through releasing low energy vibrations, we are able to fully realize our true nature on the higher end of the scale.

Simple Energy Clearing Meditation

Prepare yourself in the usual way to sit in meditation and take a couple of deep breaths in and out. Breathe deeply in and out, focusing on your breath.

Now bring your awareness to your body. Observe all the different sensations within and allow the energy creating the sensations, whether good, bad, or neutral, to release. Be present with the stuck energy without becoming involved in any way. Empty the physical body the best you can.

When you feel you are done, expand your awareness to your emotional body. Observe the emotions that surface in a detached way and allow the energy of the emotions to release.

When you are done with the emotional body, expand your awareness to your mental body. Observe, again in a detached way, and allow the energy of thoughts, beliefs, judgments, and opinions which arise to release.

Then, expand your awareness to the fourth body. This body is your link to your fundamental or soul consciousness, but is not easily accessible. Clear the physical heart of the heavy energies stuck there. Again, observe in a detached manner as the energies fall or drop away.

You will also find energy cords within the heart which connect you to others and things with which you vibrate at a complementary level, whether good or bad. Cut all these cords of attachment to everyone and everything, everywhere. These people and things will still be in your life, unless you decide to let them loose physically from your life, but you will be free of their draining and controlling energy force. These cords can also be attached to other areas of the bodies; wherever you find them, visualize severing them with a silver sword or a pair of scissors.

When done, focus on the heart chakra in the center of your chest next to the physical heart. Here you may access your soul consciousness and energy. Look for the light of your soul shining from your heart chakra. Follow it deep within. Go deeper and deeper into yourself in search of the essence of your True Self, your soul self. Be this light. Feel the amazing energy of your soul. It is uplifting and enlightening. Allow the light and energy of your soul to expand to encompass all your bodies. You will feel renewed, revitalized and you will be vibrating at a higher level of energy and consciousness.

When you are done, take a deep breath or two and open your eyes.

There are many other higher frequency "bodies," but you must take time to release lower energies and raise your consciousness and energy levels slowly, as the lower bodies need time to adjust.

18: The Law of Least Effort

How to get out of your own way

Have you ever felt stuck? I mean, really, really stuck…in the dark, not moving (forward, backwards, or sideways), confused about what to do. In this moment of confusion, you may feel afraid to do the wrong thing because you might make the situation worse.

So, rather than making a choice, you choose to be static and do nothing in the hopes that the situation will just pass.

I think we all know how that goes. Nothing changes, plus those negative feelings, reinforced by your awareness of your frustration, just get stronger. (Yes, I am going to remind you of the RAS again.)

For many of my hypnotherapy and coaching clients, this is the moment of realization that brings them to me for help.

They're stuck. They can see a better future, they can sense and feel their goal, but they just can't seem to make it happen. The harder they try, the more it eludes them.

You may feel the same way. I know that, in the past, I have.

We ask ourselves a lot of questions while in this place: "Why is so much work not leading to my intended results?" or "When will I get my break?" or "Why does nothing ever work out the way I want it to?"

You may have a few others to add to that list.

If you do, may I suggest that you DO NOT write them down this time?

It is best if you do not take action to write down these negative thoughts and ideas. The process of writing them down may help to etch them into your mind by bringing them more fully into the awareness of your RAS.

In the exercises for Chapter Fourteen, you wrote a list of negative perceptions and proceeded to seal them away. You may revisit that exercise if you wish. That process of sealing the ideas away is powerful because ultimately it is focused on the solution to the limiting ideas.

Since you now know these limiting beliefs are nothing more than the lies of ego, it's time to forget these limitations and leave them behind as you move forward, free of fear and clear on your desired outcome.

While working together through hypnotherapy, I help my clients to find their answers, align with their purpose, and discover the actions that will lead them beyond the wall they are facing.

So many times, the lessons uncovered in these sessions are things that the client already knew. They sensed what they should do, but created stories about why they should not, or could not, do anything. When they connected with their subconscious and moved away from the distracting buzz of the learned behavior of their egos, they found that they had access to all the answers that they needed.

Now, unrestricted by the limiting stories and faulty negative programming that kept them stuck, they are free, and typically excited, to begin taking action to move forward.

From this moment forward, we are going to focus on your movement.

This is when you need to become aware of the Law of Least Effort.

This Law states that when manifesting is in alignment with all Universal Laws, it will happen simply and easily. When we are in balance with our purpose, and taking intentional action, things will just seem to fall into place.

Another way to look at this Law is by remembering the quote by Roman philosopher Seneca, "Luck is what happens when preparation meets opportunity."

How do you set your goals? Do you use the SMART Goals[1] outline? It's a fine template for clarifying your intended outcome, but when we're too detailed, we actually block our flow.

Typically, these fine details come from our ego. They include things like: how much money you want to earn, the exact location of your office, or the specific person with whom you want to fall in love.

The ego conditioning shows us grand movies of how great these specific outcomes will be, and we get stuck in the film, mired in the details. When things do not happen in exactly the way our ego has presented them, we tend to feel like failures for not achieving our dreams.

When we operate from a broader vision, we see that the Universe will fill in the details. Maybe your high school or college crush married someone else…yet, when you stopped focusing on the loss of this person in your life, then you met someone else who better matched your image of a happy, healthy relationship.

The Universe had your back all along, but while you focused on the detail, you missed the other opportunities It was presenting.

Once you learned the lesson that your ideal outcome in alignment with Universal Law was not "a relationship with Person X," but instead "a happy, healthy relationship with a loving partner," then the Law of Least Effort took over.

If you are struggling, ask yourself why. Where did you lose connection to the flow?

Are you feeling fear? Maybe your bank account is running low and you do not yet see a solution on the horizon; maybe you are in a relationship that is not fulfilling you, but you think this may be your last chance at love; or maybe you are concerned that you'll never find another job that pays as well as the one you currently have... and hate...

When we're in these moments of struggle, we do not see our larger world of endless possibilities that surrounds us. Our ego keeps us focused on the small distractions that trap us in our comfort zones.

We're miserable, but at least it's a familiar place. What's outside the walls of our comfort zone is unfamiliar. That means it is scary to our ego. The ego, in its own way, is trying to protect us by keeping us in place and "safe."

When do we usually begin moving? It's actually a very simple equation. We make choices based on fear and pain.

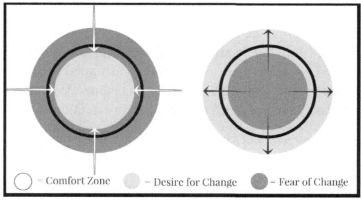

○ = Comfort Zone   ● = Desire for Change   ● = Fear of Change

© Daniel Olexa

When the fear of change is greater than our desire for change, we stay stuck with in our comfort zone. When our emotional connection to our desire for change is greater than our fear, then we begin taking action to move beyond the limits of our comfort zone.

You could also say that when the pain of being within our comfort zone is greater than the fear of change, then we will begin moving away from the discomfort of staying stuck.

I hear you thinking: "That's all fine and good, but what does it have to do with the Law of Least Effort? That all sounds like a lot of work."

And you are right. Taking that path, based in fear, moving only when we're prodded, wastes a lot of energy and time.

When we're in alignment with the Law of Least Effort, things move more easily.

We become aware that our goal is available to us, but it may not happen at exactly the time we wish it to... AND THAT'S OK. When we're operating in balance with this Law, we know that our outcomes will be delivered to us by the Universe when the time is right.

In the meantime, we do what we need to do, what we can do, to prepare ourselves for its arrival, without focusing every day on the arrival of the goal.

That's called "letting go of attachment to outcome."

Let it be. It will happen if you continue taking focused, intentional action. Trust the Universe. It is the energy of love and is the flow of abundance.

Don't worry about your result – just continue to do your diligence and work to be ready when your goal arrives.

Otherwise, what you'll attract by worrying about details is more worry and less manifestation of your goal. Focusing your energy on the event having not yet occurred will delay its arrival.

Trust is important. Connect with your Higher Self and ask if your goal is in balance with your purpose in this life.

When we connect with our higher purpose, our reason for being here in this life and on this planet, our Dharma, we can sense the flow of events in our lives.

Working within the framework of Least Resistance, we may see that each person we meet is part of a larger network. While any one of these people may not directly play a large role in our ultimate outcome, they may connect us to someone who will, or teach us a lesson that is critical to our growth and development.

EXERCISES

If you are feeling that you are struggling, step back from taking action temporarily.

Stop all you are doing and get clear.

Meditate and ask your Higher Self for information. Ask if you have been too specific, or not specific enough, in your request to the Universe.

What answers do you receive to this question? How can you adjust your point of view to see a broader perspective about your goal?

How can you let go of your attachment to the outcome and just let things flow again?

Iris' Insights

This Law epitomizes The Flow. The Law of Least Effort shows us that there is no one or no thing that is more important or unimportant than another. Everything that manifests easily and harmoniously is the truth and it is as it should be. Struggle occurs when we believe that something is not the truth or what ego conditioning dictates. The thought is that one thing is more important than another.

Source provides it all. For the most part, things are the way they are supposed to be because they fit into the harmonious pattern of nature and the Universe. Many people believe we are in control of our destiny with our thoughts, but this is only to a degree. There is the illusion that our free will and power of choice is entirely manifesting the world out there. No. We did not have to think the Universe and all things into existence. Source is existence and is the true power/creator at the same time. We can try to make something happen that we want but, as most people know, it usually does not happen and something different occurs; acceptance is key.

When we are in harmony with the Divine Will, we can understand what materializes in our lives is natural and likely. When we can look upon it with the Eye of Wisdom and either learn from it or know that it is a blessing, no matter how it may have appeared at first, we are in The Flow.

We are all but single points of energy which at times move like waves, similar to a particle wave, in one great pool of light, energy and consciousness. Ripples of energy flow through the pool and through us. If our personal flow/wave emits ripples from a stagnant pool of putrid energy within, the consequence results in problems and disharmony. If we are able to stay connected to The Flow and empty the trapped energy of ego conditioning, karma and illusion, our ripples are harmonious and balanced.

Ripples of Energy Meditation

Prepare yourself in the usual way to sit in meditation and take a couple of deep breaths in and out. Breathe deeply in and out, focusing on your breath.

Now bring your awareness to your body. Observe all the different vibrations within the body. You will notice that each sensation has its own vibration. Usually if there is pain, there is little vibration in that area. If a part of the body is pain-free, there is a sweet hum of vibration there. Imagine how each vibration travels out from your body. Is it a bumpy ripple? A smooth ripple? Is the ripple a high or low pitched one? Then visualize how these ripples

157

may be affecting others and/or what they may be creating or drawing towards you.

When you feel you are done, expand your awareness to your emotional body.

Observe all the different vibrations within the emotional body. You will notice that each emotion has its own vibration. Imagine how each emotional vibration travels outward. Is it the harsh and rough emotional ripple of anger? Is it the light and inviting ripple of love? Or is it the upsetting and scattered ripple of fear? Then visualize how these ripples may be affecting others and/or what they may be creating or drawing towards you.

When you are done with the emotional body, expand your awareness to your mental body.

Observe all the different vibrations within the mental body. You will notice that each thought, belief, judgment, and opinion has its own vibration. Imagine how each mental vibration travels outward. Is it the cutting and influential ripple of judgment? Is it the illuminated and engaging ripple of an accepting thought? Or is it the staunch and forceful ripple of an unyielding belief? Then visualize how these ripples may be affecting others and/or what they may be creating or drawing towards you.

When done with the mental body, focus in the center of your chest upon your heart chakra. Look for the light of your soul shining from your heart chakra. Follow it deep within. Go deeper and deeper into yourself in search of the essence of your True Self, your Soul Self. Feel the amazing vibration of your soul. How fast is it vibrating? What type of emotions and thoughts may be sensed within this vibration: love? compassion? joy? wisdom? acceptance? understanding? Feel the ripples of your soul vibration emitting outwards. It is inspiring and enlightening. It is all-encompassing and loving. Visualize how these ripples may be affecting others and/or what they may be creating or drawing towards you.

Stay within the heart chakra and continue to emit your soul vibrations. Your soul vibration is that of The Flow.

Remain centered there as long as you can and return to this center when you are in disharmony within and/or life is chaotic. Staying centered is the ultimate goal.

When you are done, take a deep breath or two and open your eyes.

19: The Law of Grace

Why you need to break a few eggs

The Law of Least Effort helps us to get out of our own way when we are creating struggle for ourselves and we may once again be in The Flow.

When we step back from our thoughts about a situation, and we calm ourselves through meditation or possibly self-hypnosis, we allow ourselves to become observers and we begin to see a bigger picture of how events and circumstances fit together. From this perspective, struggles once perceived by the ego are now seen as merely moments of growth as we let go of the old us and embrace our more aware self, which is who we need to be in order to manifest our desire.

I am reminded of Sisyphus.

In Greek mythology, Sisyphus was the king of Corinth. He had a reputation for being very cunning. Stories of his actions in life include earning the wrath of Zeus for revealing the location of Aegina (whom Zeus had kidnapped) to her father, Asopus.

He is also rumored to have chained Death in Hades. While Death was imprisoned, no humans died on Earth.

Yet, for all of these tales of his dubious achievements while alive, it is his fate in the afterlife for which he is best known.

As a punishment for his actions that angered the gods, Sisyphus was condemned to eternally roll a large boulder uphill in Hades. Every time Sisyphus would reach the top of the hill, the boulder would roll away from him, down to the bottom of the hill, where he would have to begin his laborious task all over again.

His story is a wonderful metaphor for how our ego perceives life: forever condemned to roll the boulder of our dreams uphill, only to see it roll away again at our moment of triumph.

Our ego conditioning keeps us small by focusing on the struggle, on the effort, on that four-letter word that is WORK, because for the ego, outside the tangible results of this job, there is only the unknown.

Ego is "afraid" of the unknown.

Instead of allowing us to explore the world outside of our comfort zone, our ego wants us to stay small and safe.

Like a baby chick still inside its egg, we remain closed off from light and flow, until we realize that we must break the shell that has protected us and kept us safe to this point in our lives.

Without taking action to peck our way out of this constricting environment, we will die.

The chicken instinctively knows that it has to get out of the egg or it will suffocate. So, it takes action to survive, and ultimately, grow.

For humans, our ego gets in the way. It tells us how great our current place is: it's safe, it's cozy, it has been so good for us, we should appreciate it and stay. Why change things, why break the walls of the home that has been so good to us? Why should we redecorate the familiar?

Our Higher Self knows why. It is because we are not meant to live a life of limitation. We are meant to grow and experience the world, bringing our unique manifestation to reality.

When we operate within the Law of Grace, we release our connection to the ego-mind. We stop listening to its thoughts of limitation.

Instead, we embrace our place with gratitude, understanding that in all struggle there are lessons to be learned that lead us to our ultimate achievement. They lead to the realization of our desire.

With grace, we happily accept that we are exactly where we are supposed to be…and all is well. That does not mean that we are complacent.

In grace, we are accepting the present as we build the future. Remember the Emotional GPS in Chapter 15?

When we are operating in balance with this Law, we also may realize that there is joy to be found in the struggle. Embracing our challenges as lessons brings us closer to achievement. Focusing with grace on what we have learned, rather than perceived punishments, brings our vibrations in tune with gratitude and continuing movement toward our path.

As we do this, we become like Sisyphus as Albert Camus envisioned him: finding absurd joy and pleasure in his work. He is an existentialist hero.

EXERCISES

As you have progressed with us through your manifestation journey, what have you learned to embrace?

What lesson is present for you as you move out of your comfort zone and toward your new self?

Iris' Insights

Grace is a divine privilege of mercy. We can invoke the Law of Grace to transmute our karmic debts and heal mentally, emotionally and physically. Through God's Grace miracles can occur and the material world can be altered. However, to realize that God's Grace is our privilege, we must work to recognize It and then act on It. Lessons must be learned and much must be surrendered before this Grace becomes available.

Each time we open our hearts to another, we are able to receive an influx of Divine Grace. Compassion, empathy, mercy, unconditional love and forgiveness are divine qualities which are our spiritual heritage. We can recognize God's Grace only when these qualities bloom within us. We need to release deeply held fear and pain to allow ourselves to heal. Then we are ready to be accepting, forgiving, compassionate and loving towards ourselves and others. We are then able to realize God's Grace and to act with God's Grace to carry out the Will of God.

EXERCISES

The prerequisite of grace is humility. No humility, no grace. We can realize God's Grace through Higher Self once we have reached a level of understanding of our soul essence. We can do this by:

- Surrendering ego conditioning – the false self, habits, thoughts, etc.
- Release desire, aversion and ignorance (delusion)
- Meditate and pray to make a higher connection
- Give of mercy and forgiveness
- Asking for forgiveness by confessing sinful attitudes and desires to those you have wronged
- Regret your wrong doing and learn from it to change

God gives grace to the humble. Practice humility by:

- Releasing arrogance
- Accept that you're not the best at everything
- Recognize your flaws
- Know that humility is not false modesty
- Avoid bragging
- Be grateful for what you have
- Accept what is

- Spend more time listening than talking. This brings a broader perspective.
- Admit when you are wrong.
- Give other people credit where credit is due.
- Ask for advice from those who have experience or knowledge that you are seeking or trying to understand.
- Compliment others for their achievements and feel genuine gladness for them.
- Do not compare yourself to others. There are always those who are better or worse off than you. Learn from this, but do not sit in judgement or be envious. They are living their lives and their fates.
- Be flexible and willing to learn from others.
- Give without glory for yourself or expectation of anything in return.
- Stop complaining. Whenever you catch yourself complaining about something, try to find two positive comments regarding the person or situation.
- Practicing patience.

20: The Law of Mentalism

Why you receive more of what you think about

As we near the end of this journey through the Universal Laws of creating and manifesting, it's time now to consider just why we manifest our lives in the ways we do.

Now please re-read that sentence.

Notice that I did not say, "why we manifest things/events/people into our lives..."

It is important that we create a clear understanding here. We manifest the whole of our lives.

Every. Single. Element.

At this moment, I'm not addressing those ideal futures and desired goals that we envision for ourselves, I'm talking about the *here and now,* the struggles, the limitations and the challenges.

Let's examine our present and how we came to be here, so that we can manifest our ideal future free from the shackles of our old selves.

In a universe of unlimited, pure potentiality, why do we experience lack rather than abundance? Why do we allow ourselves to be stressed and miserable rather than happy?

We manifested our present state of being based on our learned opinions and beliefs about the events of our past. We defined ourselves in our minds, created stories about who we are, what we are capable of and, most importantly, what we deserve.

Continuing these beliefs will create the same outcomes, both challenges and successes, in our futures.

Perhaps you are familiar with the old maxim: *"Insanity means doing the same things over and over and expecting different results."*

Do you consider yourself insane? You probably are quite rational – you're reading this book after all. You know that there is something better for you in life. You have that vision of your actualized, fulfilled life... but you aren't there yet.

There's a gap between where you are and where you want to be.

And that's frustrating.

In your frustration, what are you attracting more of?

So, if you are facing challenges; if you are not happy with your life as it is right now, I have a question for you.

Why are you creating a reality that does not bring you happiness and fulfillment?

The simple answer is because you may not believe that you are deserving of happiness.

Now you may be thinking I'm the crazy one. Of course you believe that you are deserving of happiness. Isn't everyone deserving of happiness and joy in their lives?

Yes. Everyone is deserving of creating and receiving happiness in their lives.

The important distinction here is, do they believe that they are deserving of receiving it?

Consider the story of who you tell yourself that you are.

The story that is most important to your ego identity is the story that you are creating as your life.

If you have a vision of being financially stable, successful and happy, yet you find yourself struggling to make ends meet, what stories are you telling yourself?

You may have many stories about who you are. Maybe you tell yourself that you cannot be fully happy because you are undeserving of happiness. Maybe you tell yourself that being successful comes with a price that you either don't want to pay or believe that you can't. Maybe you see yourself as a healer, a giver-to-others who cannot or should not receive monetary payment for your services.

Those are old, learned stories that are no longer serving your higher potential.

We discussed this in an earlier chapter. The Universe/God/ The Source does not tease you with visions of your life that cannot be manifested. It presents us with images of what we can achieve, who we can be when we align with It and our highest purpose, free from our limitations.

It's up to us to do the work to clear ourselves, free our minds from the prison of false-ego, embrace with gratitude all those things that caused us pain, and realize that we are perfectly who we are supposed to be. Right here, right now.

There are lessons in our pains, there are gifts in our losses. Examine those moments in your life.

The Law of Mentalism states that everything is mind. *Our thoughts create our reality.*

When you consider the daily stories in the news focusing on separation of mankind through racial division, class division, political beliefs, religious beliefs, nationalism and any other polarizing topic that can be developed, is it any wonder that we are experiencing more division and stress in the world?

Is it any surprise that we value our individual lives less? After all, in this time of stress and struggle, aren't there people more deserving than us?

We get more of what we focus our attention on.

On a profound level, this Law tells us that we are One Universal Mind. We are the All and the All is us.

If we are all One, then there is no need for division. Instead, there needs to be a realization of how our diversity creates an expanded experience for humanity.

We, as a species, are more than the sum of our parts. Our individual perspectives, when assembled together, can create a unified portrait of the world.

When separated through ego labels, we are merely individual specks of dust.

But remember this: incredibly tiny particles called atoms, when assembled with precision and intention, create the entire physical universe.

It's time to remove our limiting thoughts and beliefs. As One with the Universe, we are partners in co-creation. When we realize that all is mind and we are all part of a limitless Universe, then we may release the fears associated with lack.

As I've said before:

You are not apart from the Universe,
you are A Part of the Universe.

As children of the Universe, the abundance of the Universe is your birthright.

It's time to accept that we are loved by Creation, not punished by a playful God.

It's time to accept that we are responsible for our lives. We create what we put our minds to. Let's put our minds to positive use.

It's time to remove division and learn to play well with others, because the Universe will provide all we need for each of us. On this level, there is no competition.

It's time to be thankful for your unique you, to connect with your Divine Purpose.

How will you now change your thoughts? What will you manifest knowing that you are worthy and deserving of happiness?

How does your outlook change knowing you may be free from fear of limitation...that your true nature is abundance and everything you need is provided to you?

What do you think about that?

Now that you've seen your relationship with the Universe, it's time to bring your manifesting journey all together with the Law of Love in the next chapter.

Iris' Insights

The Law of Mentalism dictates that all of creation exists in the Mind of The Source/The Universe/God. As we are part of this The Source/The Universe/God, we are the microcosmic mind within the macrocosmic Mind. Our lives exist in our minds. Perception is reality; things are how you think they are.

"The act of observing alters the reality of being observed." (Heisenberg Principle)

From the Kybalion:

This Principle embodies the truth that 'All is Mind.' It explains that The All (which is the Substantial Reality underlying all the outward manifestations and appearances which we know under the terms of 'The Material Universe'; the 'Phenomena of Life', 'Matter', 'Energy', and, in short, all that is apparent to our material senses) is spirit which in itself is unknowable and undefinable, but which may be considered and thought of as an universal, infinite, living mind.

It also explains that all the phenomenal world or universe is simply a Mental Creation of The All, subject to the Laws of Created Things, and that the universe, as a whole, and in its parts or units, has its existence in the Mind of The All, in which Mind we 'live and move and have our being.'

There is an ineffable Oneness of all life as it is all pure consciousness. This is hard to imagine as you cannot conceptualize being consciousness.

"If the doors of perception were cleansed, everything would appear to man as it is, infinite." — William Blake

---

This quote speaks to freeing ourselves from ego conditioning and "awakening to that which we are." We cannot see the infinite, essence of our true nature. We can only remember It and be It once we are liberated from what we are not.

EXERCISES

"We are," "we have," and "we experience" what we focus on through the mind-body-soul connection. The ego mind co-creates with The Source/The Universe/God Mind as we are part of It. To know that you are part of The Source/The Universe/God, see It everywhere in everything and everyone. Keep your focus on being part of the The Source/The Universe/God and know that *You* gave *you* the ability to manifest by the very fact that you are pure energy and pure consciousness.

All is the energetic force of The Mind creating a dream in which we create our personal dreams. The dreams seem real as the microcosmic mind is essentially made to believe what is "out there" is real. Be open to what The Divine You wants you to create in your life so you can remember who you are. Know that The Divine Mind only manifests what is right, needed and best for you. It will bring amazing things you could never imagine to you, so co-creating with It is always in your best interests.

The purpose here is to know the Source Mind through the microcosmic mind to see what we are not and letting the falsity of the personal dream go. Enlightenment is the ultimate result, but not easily achieved. Only through mindfulness, meditation, renunciation (accepting that the 3-dimensional universe is impermanent and without inherent existence to be free of attachment to it) and incorporating the Laws of The Universe (Source Mind) and other methods that may aid you, can you "Know Thy Self.

21: The Law of Love

The ONE thing you need to know to realize your worthiness and achieve your dreams

How many of us grew up with the image and stories of a vengeful God from Christianity? You know the one: He watches from his throne in Heaven, judges your life and punishes you accordingly for your sins, either in this life or in the afterlife.

The metaphor of the vengeful man in the sky was created thousands of years ago to control people. It's an image that is unfortunately still promoted by those who wish to control us. Like spoiled milk, it continues to be regurgitated from the mouths of those who need to feel powerful by making others feel small.

Like Santa Claus, God in this story keeps a list. Many of us have been indoctrinated to live our lives as though we are still young children striving to be good. We are led to believe that our actions result in eternal life, that only through right action are we deserving of God's love and the rewards of Heaven.

That's a lot of pressure.

What happens when we slip up or make a mistake? We are strapped with guilt...Big "G" Guilt that says, "You should have been better," "You didn't do _____," "You don't deserve _____ anymore," and "Can't you do anything right?"

If these thoughts resonate with you, I am sorry.

This chapter is for you. Possibly more than any other entry in this book, this one is for your healing and growth.

The Law of Love is, to me, the most powerful of all the Universal Laws of Manifesting. Once we realize this truth, we can forgive ourselves and others, and know that we are part of The Source/The Universe/God.

According to this Law, Love is another word for The Source/The Universe/God. Pick the one that resonates with you.

In other words, God *is* Love. The Universe around you *is* Love. The Source of your creation *is* Love.

The Source/The Universe/God cannot *NOT* love. That is an ego-driven personification created to separate humanity from our connection to Source.

Think of it this way. Much like a parent, if our Source can give love, then it can also withhold love. Thus, the story of living to uphold a certain code becomes the norm.

By creating God as an entity outside of us, we become separated from our knowledge of our worthiness. Rather than understanding that *we are a part of the whole of creation,* we see ourselves instead as *apart from* creation.

Love creates. Love supports. Love challenges us to grow and become our best selves.

Much like a fish swimming in the ocean is unaware of the water in which it is living, we are sometimes blind to the nature of our environment.

The Universe Supports Our Existence

Consider this: How many events had to take place in order to create your presence on this earth at this time? Your parents had to meet. Prior to that they had to be born, prior to that, their parents had to be born and meet, and so on, and so on.

Generations of your ancestors had to be born, live long enough to meet and procreate to pass their DNA and cultural stories to you. You are the unique embodiment of this lineage. If you choose to have children, they will carry your story forward in their unique way.

Now consider that this is true for every one of the 7.6 billion people on planet Earth at this moment. It has been true since the first humans evolved and will continue to be true as our species continues to procreate.

How many events have occurred in your life that have brought you to this exact moment? Have you ever had a brush with death – a moment where you feared for your life and survived? What blessings have been granted to you by family, friends, and perhaps strangers, that have impacted your outlook on life?

How has your past experience created your beliefs regarding what you can achieve in this life? What cultural or familial seas are you swimming in, unaware of how they are shaping your attitudes and beliefs?

It is from this place that our sense of what we deserve is imprinted on us. Cultural norms, gender roles, religious dogma, and obligations to family structures are just a few droplets in this vast ocean.

Awareness of this metaphorical sea does not mean that you are beholden to it. The beliefs and practices of our ancestors may no longer have a practical place in our modern lives. When we realize that we are swimming in a sea that no longer serves our growth, it is our responsibility to evolve, grow legs, and begin walking on land.

Just as The Universe supported the evolution of water-based life moving to land, it will support you in your evolution.

It is important that I again remind you that this does not mean the process will be easy. You will be challenged to grow and change further to exist and succeed in this new environment.

Your ego will expect things to be easy. It will look for shortcuts based on its ideas of the way things should be.

When we become aware of such things as the Law of Attraction, we tend to approach these Laws as spoiled children, repeatedly saying, "I want, I want, I want...."

When the Universe doesn't deliver our desire in the way that we want it to be, we further separate, treating the Universe as a negligent parent. If it won't give us what we want, then we'll withhold our love for it, act out for attention and blame it for not loving us.

We act like petulant children. That's ego conditioning.

And that's how we lose our way.

Reconnecting with Love is the way back.

Accepting that we're responsible for our lives is the first step. The Universe is always delivering what we're asking it for, but how many of us know exactly what we are asking for?

Attraction, Vibration, Polarity, Cause and Effect, these Laws and the remaining 16 Laws in this book all work in coordination to manifest our lives. We create our lives as the story of what we think we deserve.

When we embrace the Law of Love, we can finally know, in our hearts and souls, that we deserve far more than our ego-minds will ever conceive. Living beyond the limitations of our ancestral stories and ego-driven beliefs, we can connect to our unique purpose, our Dharma.

That goal you have in your thoughts... You know the one, that goal that's so big it's scary and at the same time gives you butterflies of excitement as you cringe at its scope? The one that you tell yourself, "I could never do that." It's a gift from the Universe.

That idea has been given to you in Love. In the highest sense, Love is the greatest gift. You are part of The Source/The Universe/God which is Love. Therefore, you are love, and at the same time, you are loved.

Be and use this love to manifest your ideal life.

Oh, it will take work to achieve. The Law of Least Effort can help you understand how to co-create more efficiently, but don't you feel better already knowing that when you take action to achieve it, the Universe "has your back"?

If our Source *is* Love, then our connection to love is universal and eternal. In this light, manifesting is no longer about our behavior in the eyes of The Source/The Universe/God. In a universe of love, the realization of our goals is our birthright.

Here is the one thing you need to know to realize your connection to Source: You are the energy of love. You are loved and deserving.

How can I say that? Because as a part of a Universe filled with the energy of love, your birthright is abundance, which is the expression of the flow of this energy.

Here is the Truth for you to consider:

1. The Source/The Universe/God is infinite/everything.

2. The Source/The Universe/God is the energy of Pure Love.

3. You are a part of The Source/The Universe/God, If God is infinite and everything, that includes you. You are not separate from "everything."

4. Therefore, you are the embodiment of Love. You are infinitely deserving and loved.

How does it feel to know that you are Love?

Love Creates

Love is the highest vibration of all.

EXERCISES:

It's time to quiet the negative voices of ego and move forward to re-connect with The Universe/God/Source.

Focus on your goal. Imagine it as fully realized in the present moment. How does that feel?

What positive thoughts come to you? Are there any negative thoughts or fears that come up?

Examine any negative emotions. Ask why they are there. Where did they come from? Where did you learn these fears?

Thank them for being present. They have worked to protect a part of you from an imagined threat. They've done their job and now it's time to move beyond them. You no longer need these limitations. Quiet any such thoughts as though you were guiding a baby to sleep: gently and with love.

Now go grab your dream!

Iris' Insights

This Love, we cannot actually know or understand in the true sense. This Love is unconditional (without ego conditions). It is free of wants, lust or personal truths. This Love is what we are, as It is the energy force of life itself and creation.

This Law states that this is The Way, The Light, as It is God Itself. All is One within this Love. This is the highest Law and the key to everything, as God's Love is the highest vibration which creates the "environment" for All to be.

We can know that we are this Love once we surrender the false self and become non-attached to the outside world. After this, we begin to know ourselves as soul, the essence of our true nature which is this Love. It is the surrender of ego conditioning and freedom from its control over us that allows us to be this Love.

Mindfulness of the Love of God

The force of the Love of God is in everything and everyone and creates All That Is. Yet, It is beyond time or space. Therefore, it is found most fully in the now.

If we are able to step back and be the observer, we can use our ability of mindfulness to reach a state of release of thoughts and emotions without being affected by them. Mindfulness of all senses and the reactions of the body and ego-based thoughts and emotions allow us to realize the exact moment any of these emerge. We can then examine whether the thoughts, emotions or reactions of the body is of ego-conditioned mind (it is all about the "me") or of a higher state of mind (loving kindness). As we stay in the moment of observation, the sub- or un-conscious reactive thoughts, emotions and bodily sensations are disabled as they "float" by harmlessly. We then see the facts of what is in that moment and we are able to understand our motivations and whether they are of ego-conditioned or of higher mind. We have clear knowing of the moment at which time we are most often able to connect with the Love of God, our true divine natural energy, and be guided by It.

As this Love is unconditional, it cannot be conceptualized. It can only be recognized. We can start realizing the Love by acting the way we believe God may act or perform what we believe God would want us to do without harming anyone or anything. This is the moment of higher knowing.

Or we may imitate the actions of someone we admire of higher mind such as the Dalai Lama, a true yogi or guru, such as Deepak Chopra.

When this Love wells up within us, it brings us into the throws of ecstasy. This Love also connects us with the love we have for God, that indefinable being-ness, that ultimate power that is Love as we are one-and-the-same with It.

We know we have realized this Love when we have acquired great devotion toward The Source/The Universe/God. It is all that matters. When we are able to awaken to being this Love, we realize that the great journey of becoming That over many, many lifetimes has been a struggle for naught, as we have always been Divine Love.

Acknowledgements

Iris and I would like to thank Norma-Jean Strickland for her providing her wonderful insights as our editor. Her familiarity with this topic was instrumental in guiding us to clarify our thoughts to present in the best way to you, our readers.

Thank you as well to all of the members of our Facebook group, Practical Manifesting Insiders.

Appreciation is also due to our many readers who gave us feedback on early drafts of this manuscript. Your suggestions helped us to make this the best possible presentation of all of the practical aspects of manifesting that are normally ignored in this genre.

Finally, with much gratitude, we would like to thank The Source for enlightening us with this idea and providing us with the tools to bring it into reality.

A Pessimist's Guide to Manifesting

About the Authors

Daniel Olexa has been drawn to the powers of the mind for his entire life. After realizing his passion for helping others to improve their lives and his natural ability at problem solving, Daniel left the corporate world and began his studies in hypnotherapy. After completing 500 hours of training at the Institute of Interpersonal Hypnotherapy in Tampa, Florida, Daniel opened his first practice in Naples, FL.

Daniel continues to empower others around the world to realize their strengths, discover The Flow, and reinvent their lives from his current office in Los Angeles, CA.

He is the vice-president of the Long Beach Chapter of the Holistic Chamber of Commerce.

Orecia (Iris) Irene Terner originally hails from Edmonton, Alberta and now resides in Victoria, British Columbia, Canada. Iris studied under Randall Chipps, an aboriginal Medicine Man and Chieftain of the Dhididat Tribe of the Nootka people of the Pacific West Coast. Randall discovered Iris to be a natural-born shaman who would carry on his legacy. Upon completing her education through Randall's accredited integrated school, Iris has been working as a Shaman, Behavior Therapist, spiritual teacher, and Reiki Practitioner/Teacher for over 20 years. Iris lives The Flow which this book describes in detail.

A Pessimist's Guide to Manifesting

Chapter Notes

Chapter 8

1. https://jamesclear.com/delayed-gratification

Chapter 11

1. http://content.time.com/time/magazine/article/0,9171,1580438,00.html

Chapter 17

1. https://ed.ted.com/lessons/just-how-small-is-an-atom

2. http://www.pbs.org/wgbh/nova/blogs/physics/2013/08/the-good-vibrations-of-quantum-field-theories/

Chapter 18

1. https://www.smartsheet.com/blog/essential-guide-writing-smart-goals

A Pessimist's Guide to Manifesting

Further Resources

Buettner, Dan. *The Blue Zones*. National Geographic, 2010.

Chopra, Deepak. *The Seven Laws of Spiritual Success,* New World Library / Amber-Allen Publishing, 1994.

Dean, James, and Eric Litwin. *I Love My White Shoes.* Harper Collins, 2010.

Gaines, Edwene. *The Four Spiritual Laws of Prosperity.* Rodale Books. 2005

Gawdat, Mo. *Solve for Happy.* North Star Way. 2017.

Hankel, Isaiah. *Black Hole Focus.* Capstone. 2014.

Intelligent Change. *The Five Minute Journal.* Intelligent Change, Inc. 2013

Seligman, Martin. *Learned Optimism.* Vintage. 2006.

Three Initiates. *The Kybalion: A Study of The Hermetic Philosophy of Ancient Egypt and Greece.* Rough Draft Printing. 2012.

54415263R00104

Made in the USA
Columbia, SC
30 March 2019